Letter from
Vienna

A Daughter
Uncovers
Her Family's
Jewish Past

Claudia Cornwall

Foreword by Raul Hilberg

Douglas & McIntyre
Vancouver/Toronto

Douglas & McIntyre
1615 Venables Street
Vancouver, British Columbia
V5L 2H1

Canadian Cataloguing in Publication Data
Cornwall, Claudia Maria.
Letter from Vienna
ISBN 1-55054-115-3
1. Cornwall, Claudia Maria.   2. Weiner family.
3. World War, 1939–1945 – Concentration camps.
4. Jews – Austria – Biography.   I. Title.
D804.3.C67 1995   940.53'18'0922   C95-910032-6

Editing by Barbara Pulling
Book design by Linda Gustafson/Counterpunch
Cover photograph by Willy Frensdorff of Lore and Walter Wiener,
    Tunsin Road, Shanghai, 1946

Printed in the United States of America

The publisher gratefully acknowledges the assistance of the Canada Council and of the British Columbia Ministry of Tourism, Small Business and Culture for its publishing programs.

For my family

Contents

Foreword

She was born in Shanghai, China, where she was baptized in the Anglican Church, and she grew up in Vancouver, the tranquil Canadian city on the Pacific Ocean. She has lived in the Vancouver area ever since, forming a family and taking part in the usual activities of the middle class to which she belongs. Yet Claudia Cornwall would not have been born in a Chinese city, where her parents had met, and she would not have been brought to Vancouver, had there not been an assault that ripped into her father's and mother's lives in the Greater German Reich of Adolf Hitler. There, in the heart of Europe, far removed from eastern China or western Canada, she found her roots.

When Claudia Cornwall was a child, she did not hear much about what had been done to her parents. They belonged to a relatively silent group of victims. It was as a mature adult that she made her discoveries. What she learned, and even more the process of her investigation, form the contents of this account.

Silence as such is not unknown. Notably among the perpetrators it was rather common. Not a few participants in the actions of the Nazi regime went to their graves without a word about "those times." One can understand their reticence, given the postwar outcry about their deeds, and one can also see why some of their offspring have turned to personnel records, articles or books for revelations. But the child of victims? Why should *she* have to throw herself into a long and arduous search? What did *her* parents have to hide? That they really *were* victims?

Claudia Cornwall was to be protected from the past, particularly in her childhood, lest she be hurt and possibly debilitated. The Jews of Germany, and later those of Austria under German control, had been targeted under a cascade of decrees. They were subjected to derision, dismissals, despoliation and segregation. Any German national, regardless of religious persuasion, who had at least three Jewish grandparents was affected by these anti-Jewish measures. Any half-Jew who did not belong to the Jewish religion and was not married to a Jewish partner could still lose an array of opportunities. In this bewildering situation, some Jews tried to hold on, believing themselves to be safe by virtue of some "essential" job or advancing age, but most of those who did not emigrate were destined to perish. Others who left at the last moment were lucky to be refugees or flotsam out of German reach.

The Jews of Germany and Austria spoke the German language, which for most of them was their mother tongue. They were going to feel the trauma of an outcast, whether

they stayed or departed. Some of these Jews lost not only possessions and homes but also self-esteem. They were ashamed,
not for anything they might have done but for what had happened to them. Although many victims rediscovered and
embraced half-forgotten Jewish traditions, a number of others attempted to jettison precisely those customs as ballast. A
few changed their religion, detaching themselves from fellow
victims as much as possible. Yet in their private lives the
Christians of Jewish background could not always find new
anchors. Just as survivors quickly sought mates among other
survivors after the liberation, so refugees married refugees,
and baptized victims formed unions with their counterparts.
Only one certainty might arise in their thoughts: the recollection of humiliation and anxiety was not to be passed on to
the next generation. The children were to be "free."

During the postwar era there was not much demand for
memoirs of persecutees. Survivors and refugees, like the veterans of battlefronts, were advised to forget what they had
suffered and witnessed. The whole tenor of the time was
focussed on betterment. The future had to be built, and
rewards awaited those who could throw themselves whole-
heartedly into the work. In the Western world a new align-
ment had been formed, with a place reserved for Germany,
against the Soviet Union. As new issues and crises preempted
attention, the recent Holocaust was enveloped in a haze, and
prevailing sentiment, approaching a taboo, discouraged much
delving into the catastrophe. Then the Cold War decayed, and
the Holocaust was to be seen clearly in more and more detail.

Now it turned out that secrecy, camouflage and vagueness
had not protected the adults who had been born into the families of victims. What had emerged from repression was the
need to know. Awareness of one's origins was not dispensable
after all. The universal question "Whose child am I?" or

"Whose grandchild?" is asked not merely about the identity of forebears; it is a probe to ascertain the nature of their dilemmas and decisions. Answers to such queries may come easily to long-established citizens. But in Claudia Cornwall's case the quest was a major task that took years. She had to approach the problem somewhat like a detective confronted by a mystery, with painstaking perusal of private correspondence and unsparing questioning of members of her family. She immersed herself in archival records and walked in a street where one pair of her grandparents had lived and from where these two people had disappeared. She wanted to know what had happened to them. Her search became a drama, the drama a record, the record this book.

At the end, her widowed mother says, "We are who we are." With these ambiguous words, she allows her daughter to find herself.

Raul Hilberg

Adalbert Wiener
1848 — ca. 1920

married

Luise Mautner
1851 — ca. 1890

six other children

Rudolf Wiener
1874 — 1942

married

Regine Moldau
1880 — 1942

four other children

Family Tree

Wiener/
Frensdorff

Eduard Frensdorff
1854 — 1908

married

Bertha Löwenstein
? — ca. 1932

Arthur Frensdorff
1876 — 1940

Helmut Frensdorff
ca. 1885 — 1938

Clara Frensdorff
1877 — 1941

Wilhelm Frensdorff
1881 — 1947

married

Joseph Marholz
1858 — 1927

married

Anna Härtl
? — 1900

Melitta Marholz
1887 — 1978

three other children

and after,
married

Hedwig v. Klingspor
1874 — ca. 1965

Kurt Marholz
1905 — 1984

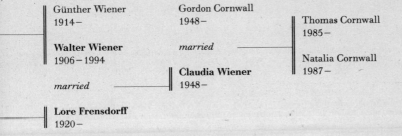

Günther Wiener
1914–

Gordon Cornwall
1948–

Thomas Cornwall
1985–

Walter Wiener
1906–1994

married

Natalia Cornwall
1987–

married

Claudia Wiener
1948–

Lore Frensdorff
1920–

Anna Döltl,
Walter Wiener
and Regine
Wiener,
around 1910

The Christmas Card

A woman with thick white hair and grey-green eyes is sitting at a white desk in a white room holding a white phone. Her skin is pale, the translucent ivory of a former redhead. This is my mother. I am at the other end of the line, a dark curly-haired woman with the same grey-green eyes. I am sitting on a blond cane chair in front of a bookshelf, holding a red phone. It is January 1989.

"Did you know?" I ask. I expect her to say that she did not.

"Yes," she answers instead.

"Why didn't you tell me?"

"If I have to choose between my loyalty to Daddy and my loyalty to you, Daddy comes first," my mother explains. "He never wants to talk about it. But now the Pandora's box is open."

I am calling because of a Christmas card I received the day before from my Uncle Günther in Vienna. On the front was a photograph taken in the Tyrolese Alps showing a church and snow and sunshine. When I opened the card, I found another photograph inside. This one was of my father at about the age of four. He was standing in a garden between two women, holding their hands. He gazed straight at the camera with a solemn expression.

I took the picture out of the card and laid it down, thinking I would frame it and hang it on my bedroom wall. Then I began to read my uncle's message. Writing in English, he opened with warm wishes and news about his family. There was nothing in his friendly tone or his remarks to prepare me for one sentence in the middle of his note. He offered it without explanation or comment. Then he went on to express the hope that our two families would meet in Austria for a holiday soon. He told me that a pacemaker implanted in my aunt's heart made her feel much better and sent us all his love and many kisses.

I stared back at the photograph. Again I saw three people in a garden nearly eighty years ago. One of the women was crouching. She wore a dark dress and a starched apron. On her lap were three picture books. The other woman stood. Around her shoulders was a printed shawl. Her dress was dark too, but the apron covering it was not so crisp. She smiled. I noticed the sunflowers, already tall but without their heads. The time was probably midsummer. As my father was born in July, perhaps the occasion was his birthday and the books I saw were presents.

I returned to the note. My uncle's rivetting sentence was only twelve words long. He had written, "The lady standing up was our mother, who died in concentration camp." I had never heard about this. Ever.

I decided not to hang the photograph of my father and his mother on my bedroom wall. It made me uneasy. How would I speak about it to visitors? Should I say, "Yes, that's my grandmother and my father. In Austria, many years ago — on a summer vacation." Or, "My grandmother, you know; she died in a concentration camp." I put the picture back inside my uncle's Christmas card and returned the card to its envelope. Later I would place the envelope in a metal filing cabinet, but first it would sit by the phone for a couple of weeks.

Now, while talking to my mother about my uncle's note, I reach for it. Pulling out the photograph, I look at my grandmother's face. I notice her dark humorous eyes under their arched eyebrows. "Was she Jewish?" I ask.

"Yes," my mother replies.

"Was that why Daddy and Günther left Vienna?"

"Yes," she says again.

I have always felt that my father did not want to talk to me about his parents. My mother has told me most of what I know about them. I am beginning to understand why I felt so uncomfortable raising the subject with him.

I know that my grandmother was born in Poland, that her first name was Regine and that she was a good cook. My father still speaks of the blueberry *Buchteln* (small buns) she used to make. But beyond that is a blank. Now I feel as though she had died twice — first, somewhere in Eastern Europe, and secondly, in our heads, by not being remembered. I certainly had no idea she was Jewish. My father never observed any Jewish traditions or customs. I was baptized an Anglican and brought up in a vaguely Christian way. We always had a Christmas tree and presents but never went to church.

"What about my grandfather? Was he Jewish too?" I ask.

"Not completely, I think," my mother says. This stuns me again: there were Jewish relatives on both sides of my father's family.

My mother's answers to my questions are short and direct. Normally our conversations are much more discursive. I can ask her whether I should give my father a bird feeder as a present and within seconds find that we are talking about rats or the economy. But today there are no digressions and I miss them. I find myself wanting associations — a context — to help me make sense of what is happening. For once my mother provides none.

There is a part of my father I know nothing about. I wonder if he went to a synagogue as a young man. Did he have a bar mitzvah? When did he begin to celebrate Christmas? Was it strange to do so?

"Did my grandfather die in a camp too?" I want to know.

"I think he died before the war," my mother says. I feel relieved.

On a slushy Saturday afternoon a few days later, I visit my parents, Lore and Walter Wiener. Although I debate whether to phone ahead or not, in the end I just go. We live about half an hour apart by car. As I drive across the two bridges and through the downtown streets that separate us, I realize I am nervous. I do everything slowly and deliberately. I make certain all my car doors are locked when I park. Going down my parents' front walk, I look back at the water pooling in the footprints I leave in the wet snow.

My father opens the door for me. He is over eighty and slightly stooped. His eyes are blue and his hair, once dark blond, is now white. He smiles. "Where are the kids?" "With Gordon," I say. Still standing in the front hall, still wearing my coat, I bring out the photograph. "Your brother sent it to me." Then I hug my father. I feel his shoulder blades through his morning gown. He must have just had his afternoon nap, I think. "He told me what happened to your mother, I am so sorry." He takes the photograph, examines it closely, looks back at me and says, "Oh, you mean the Holocaust."

We sit down in the living room and my mother joins us. "Perhaps I should have warned him," she says to me. But, to my surprise, my father does not seem distressed about what I have discovered. For the first time that I can remember, he speaks to me at length about his family. He tells me about his paternal grandfather, Adalbert Wiener, who lived on a large farm and had seven children. My father's father, Rudolf, was the oldest. "I don't know what happened to these people," my father says.

We drink tea. The sky grows dark. Then my father talks about his mother's sister, Susanne. "She was married to Max Bergmann, a furniture dealer who sold goods on credit. One day, some of his customers came into the building and threw him down an elevator shaft. He survived, but after that, the whole Bergmann family committed suicide. They turned on the gas in their place." Max and Susanne, their son Alfred, their daughter Lotte, and a grandson about five or six years old all died.

"When did it happen?" I ask.

"The Germans came in the middle of March 1938. It was shortly after that."

"My mother's brother, Max Moldau," my father continues, "managed to get to England with the help of the Freemasons. My mother had hoped to be able to go to relatives in England too, but it didn't work out."

It is night now and cold. I have one more question to ask before I go. "Were your parents practising Jews?"

"My mother was."

"And your father?"

My father shrugs. "He went to the synagogue perhaps once a year for something like Yom Kippur."

I drive home along Vancouver's wet streets. The storm sewers are plugged with half-melted snow, and near the curbs the puddles are deep. Water smacks against the doors of my car. I am thinking about that spring, over half a century ago, when it started, when Austria became part of the Reich. Were the early flowers blooming along the Danube River? Were the leaves on the trees small and bright green? Was my father able to take any pleasure in such things?

Willy Frensdorff and crew, June 8, 1927

I Have to Tell You Something

June 8, 1927. The *Juno II* leaned into a moderate breeze under an overcast sky. The captain, my mother's father, Hans Martin Wilhelm Frensdorff, lay comfortably on deck in his shirt-sleeves. Two other men sat beside him conversing. They had just won a sailing race around Helgoland, a small island off Germany's north coast. After eight hours at sea, they were heading into port – the Weser Yacht Club at Lemwerder. A story about this event appeared in a local newspaper, the *Bremer Nachrichten*. A photograph of it hangs in my parents' front hall, immediately to your left as you walk in the door. Another copy, which my parents gave to my son, Thomas, hangs in my house, also in the front hall, to your right as you enter.

We have an engraved silver cigarette case, too. Under the lid, it says, "*Nordseewoche, Helgoland, 1927, 1. Preis*" (North

Sea Week, Helgoland, 1927, First Prize). No one in our family smokes any more, but Thomas keeps a treasured silver dollar inside.

My maternal grandfather died a year before I was born. But I always felt I was better acquainted with him than with my father's parents. I knew that he had been born in Hamburg, as had his two brothers, Arthur and Helmut, and his sister, Clara. He was an electrical engineer who had worked for the Aktiengesellschaft Weser, a shipyard in Bremen. He was innovative: some of his ideas were patented. My mother had told me how he had kept his job, even during the worst of the Depression. He had been given a slip of paper that stated he could be dismissed at any time without notice, but the Ag. Weser had never let him go.

As a kid, I used to wear my grandfather's leather sailing jacket with the brown quilted sleeves. There was a very old movie camera that was his, too. I could turn the handle, make a clicking sound and pretend I was a director. And sometimes I would take out his medals from the First World War. The bronze-and-iron cross he was given for his service as an X-ray technician lay in a navy-blue box.

Now, when my son announces triumphantly, "We won World War I!" I remonstrate gently, "I don't know who 'we' is. My grandfather was slogging it out on the other side." My son is puzzled. He thinks a bit and says a shade less triumphantly, "The Canadians won!"

My favourite picture of my grandfather is one he gave my grandmother, Melitta Josephine Marholz, before they were married. He wears his hair parted in the middle and has round wire-rimmed glasses like those that became fashionable in the sixties. His collar is high, white and stiff, and on the print, across the shoulder of his well-cut suit, is the inscription, "Your old loyal Willy."

But I am not as well acquainted with my grandfather as I thought. I learn this one afternoon while I am sitting in the car with my mother. We have just had lunch and I have driven her to the store my parents own. It is three days after I talked to my father about his brother's note.

"Did your parents know any of this story about Daddy?" I ask my mother.

"My father did. My mother didn't, at least not when we first married, because only the occasional Red Cross letter got through."

That winter afternoon, my hands, which rest on the steering wheel, are gloved. I am wearing a green coat with a blue wool lining. My mother is wearing a white wool coat with curly lambskin inside and white boots. The day is raw; a slurry of ice and water nearly four inches deep lies on the street outside. Although the engine is turned off, it is still warm in the car. I am reluctant to get out.

My mother begins talking about 1933. She was thirteen and Hitler had been chancellor since the end of January. One day my grandmother said to her, "I have to tell you something about your father."

Like me, my mother was an only child. When my grandmother was pregnant, she and my grandfather had expected a boy. They had only one name ready — Klaus. Although the baby turned out to be a girl, my grandparents were not disappointed. Before my grandfather drove to the Herrenhausen Clinic in Hanover to pick up his wife and child, he stuffed the back seat of the car full of cherry blossoms. My mother's basket nestled among them on the ride back to Osnabrück, where they lived. It was April 9, 1920. An open car. The baby called Lore Maria came home in a haze of flowers.

What my grandmother had to say that day in 1933 did not change how my mother felt about her father. But she did not tell any of her friends what she learned. As the years passed, she rarely mentioned it to anyone. "According to the Nazis," my grandmother had explained, "your father is Jewish."

In sixty-six years, the words have not lost their capacity to surprise. I am startled and unsure of myself. When will the stories stop? What else has not been told?

My mother was baptized a Lutheran. At fourteen, she was confirmed during a ceremony held in Bremen's St.-Petri-Dom, the old cathedral in the centre of the city. "I remember the dress I wore. I made it myself out of white crepe romaine. It was very intricate, with horizontal tucks," my mother says.

My mother's family always celebrated Christmas. I had often heard her recollections of the holidays in their first house in Bremen, on Isarstrasse. On Christmas Eve, my mother would pace impatiently upstairs, wearing her best dress, her bright red hair brushed, her freckled face washed. "When will it be time?" she'd wonder. Finally six o'clock would arrive. A bell would ring and she'd race down the stairs. Her parents would slide open the white panelled doors leading to the dining room. There it was — the tree, candlelit and decorated with silver tinsel. The unwrapped presents lay around its base.

My grandfather would cook the dinner, although normally he did not set foot in the kitchen. On this night the meal was fish, however. Willy had grown up in northern Germany where seafood was a popular staple, but my grandmother was from Austria, where it was not. "I think because it was such a ceremonial occasion, my daddy thought he should cook it," my mother explains, "to be sure it was right."

The story of how my mother celebrated Christmas, how her Christmas Eve dinner was always fish and how her father always cooked it, was part of my Christmas as a child. It has become part of my children's Christmas too, part of the melange of traditions that my husband, Gordon, and I follow. On December 24, there are presents at my parents' house and a seafood dinner, usually prawns. Later, we go to a large party at my mother-in-law's. There is a tree with real candles. They are lit only once, as a special treat. Christmas morning, my son, Thomas, and my daughter, Talia, go into our living room to see what Santa has brought. One year, Thomas chuckled as he shook the contents of his stocking onto the floor. "He always brings us an orange and he *always* puts it in the toe."

My father never told me stories about his Christmases, but I didn't find that odd. I didn't ask him how he celebrated the occasion or what his favourite memories were. Now I think it strange that those questions never occurred to me.

"When in 1933 did you find out about your father?" I ask my mother as we sit side by side, looking through the sleet-spattered windshield.

"I don't know. I only remember that we were downtown on a street somewhere. Maybe it was near the Dom."

"Were you frightened?"

"I don't think so," my mother says. "I suppose it really didn't sink in. I knew my father wasn't like the Greenbergs who lived across the street and went to the synagogue every week. He was my daddy. He was German – he was born in Hamburg."

"How could it not sink in?" I want to know. My mother is not able to explain. She guesses. "Maybe it was my age." And then she adds, "I never felt Jewish. I remember going on holidays and seeing park benches with signs, 'Jews Not Allowed.' We always sat on them anyway. And once when we were visiting Heidelberg, walking around the university, I remember how the students greeted my father. They said, '*Heil, Alter Herr*' [Hello, sir]. Then, I supposed they were taking him for

11

one of their professors, with his very white hair, although this was already in the Nazi time, when there weren't any Jewish professors. Now, I think they might have been regarding him as an alumnus. In any case, I know he was pleased to be addressed that way."

Later, I will not remember getting out of the car following this conversation. I won't remember what I did for the rest of the afternoon. I know that eventually I came home and told my husband. I don't remember what he said. But from time to time I think how strange it is that my mother and I should have made similar discoveries – she at thirteen and I at forty.

I struggle to make sense of what I have heard. During the next few months, I have nightmares: in one, I dream that I am Jewish and in Nazi Germany. I wake up in the middle of the night, almost paralyzed with fear. I have to go to the bathroom but the prospect of getting out of bed terrifies me. I haven't felt this way since I was a child afraid of lions hiding in the darkness.

In my diary I write, "It is interesting that I should have so much fear. I wonder where it comes from. I remember that when I asked my mother whether my paternal grandfather was Jewish, she said, 'Not completely, I think.' And I didn't *want* him to be. What are all these strange feelings?"

By the fall of 1989, I have formed the idea of writing a book, but it doesn't begin easily. I record my initial difficulties. "Blocked. I have been trying to write what is supposed to be the first chapter. I have the first two pages and then for some reason the flow stops."

It is as if I am not ready to absorb this new knowledge. For a long time, I don't even read anything about the war years. However, in the spring of 1990, I begin browsing through my local library. I come across Martin Gilbert's *The*

Holocaust. Poring over his detailed account, which mentions many individuals, I find myself hoping to see something about my relatives. But their names do not appear.

I am groping, not even sure of what I should be trying to find. Early in the summer, I decide to refresh my memory of the afternoon when my mother told me what she had learned in 1933. I get out my diary, a student's exercise book, lined, with a blue cover. I am especially interested in the emotions I had then. The January 11, 1989, entry starts, "Well, the saga of my family continues." I read on eagerly. "So now I am three-quarters Jewish. Or not? My mother says Judaism is a religion, not a race. So as I have never practised...?" The tone is detached and sometimes ironical. I see the words, "It's all very curious. You get to be forty and there still are surprises in store!" About my maternal grandmother, I wrote, "So far, no revelations about her. Perhaps she will turn out to be the long-lost Princess Anastasia of Russia."

Disappointed that there is so little about my feelings, I am just about to put the notebook away when a few sentences catch my eye. Jotted there in blue ink is, "His ancestors had converted to Lutheranism. However, although he could produce what my father could not — a birth certificate from a parish — it wasn't 'good enough.'"

I reread this reference to my mother's father several times. I find it so interesting because now I know it is not true. I have learned that my grandfather's ancestors did not convert to Lutheranism. It was he who did. Like my father, he would not have been able to produce a birth certificate from a parish, only a baptism certificate.

So my understanding was faulty. How did this come about? Did my mother somehow mislead me? Did I manage to misinterpret her? Is this what happens when ideas "don't sink in"? Interested in my own thought processes, I continue to look through my diary. I see I first mentioned my grandfather's conversion about sixteen months after that snowy afternoon when my mother and I talked in the car. In April 1990, I wrote, "W.F. was born in Jewish faith and turned as a young man. Became Lutheran to have better chance of promotion. (Around 1900, during time of obligatory military service.)" I was apparently unaware of the discrepancy between this and what I thought to be true earlier; I did not allude to it.

Now I know that even this April diary entry is not quite right. Since making these notes, I have found my grandfather's baptism certificate among my parents' papers. Witnessed by his brother, Arthur, the ceremony took place at St. Johannis Church in Harvesthude, then a small village outside Hamburg. The date was September 22, 1912. It was just six weeks before he married my grandmother, Melly. Born in Vienna to a Catholic family, she became Lutheran too. I had always known this but I had assumed she wanted to conform to her husband's beliefs. I had not realized their conversion was mutual. Evidently my mother hadn't either. "Don't you think your father converted because he was going to marry?" I asked her when I found the certificate. "You know," she said, "I never discussed it with him."

I suppose my mother was speculating when she told me that her father had become a Lutheran in 1900 during his year of military service. How had I missed her uncertainty?

Walter Wiener's student card, University of Vienna, 1926-30

When Even Dogs Wore the Swastika

"I think I am scared of the display of feelings. I circle around emotions, come gradually closer, circling all the time," I write in my diary on July 4, 1990. "The circles get tighter and tighter. But it goes slowly."

The following day I recall that as a young man my father had written poems. Several years before, I had found one of these in an old black lacquer chest in my parents' dining room. I had asked a printer to reproduce it on vellum paper with a letterpress. Then I'd framed it and given it to my father for Christmas.

At the time, I'd seen other poems too, penned on yellowed brittle paper in that unfamiliar hand – my father's as a young man. But they were hard to read and I had left them rolled up in the trunk, tied with a purple ribbon. Now I go back to the trunk. I find a poem written in Vienna, dated March 1938. This was the month that German troops, accompanied by Adolph Hitler himself, entered my father's native Austria. But the poem is not about that. Translated from German, it reads:

A small space with delicate things,
Skillfully arranged in many corners.
In front of the window a soft curtain
Keeps dreams from waking –
Dreams that sleep in this room,
Dreams filled with the secrets
Of a painful, deep longing
For life in all its strange confusion
For feelings that endure.
Feelings that we poor stupid men
Call by so many names.
A small space with a colourful richness,
All its humanity
Has become a dear friend.

As I read the poem, I take the description of the room to be a metaphor. The dear friend sheltering dreams is Vienna, the city my father loves and will leave six months later. When I mention this interpretation to my father, he says, "It was a real room. I was tutoring a young woman, in English, I think. It was her room, where we studied. She was pretty and flirtatious." He lapses into silence. "In hindsight, though," I say, "couldn't you see it as a description of Vienna?" He shrugs.

Some of the poems are in a booklet with a tattered purple cover on which my father has printed the word *Gedichte* (Poems). He bought the notebook at the stationer's next door to his place at 108 Hietzinger Hauptstrasse. "I think the name of the shop was Mitterbacher," he says. "It was the kind of notebook that students used for their lessons in those days." The earliest poem is dated Summer 1925.

> *The rain falls restlessly,*
> *My thoughts flow into infinite space,*
> *Ideas, feelings rush by,*
> *Longing is caressing me with painful love,*
> *The wonder of life asks me for an answer...*

Now it is also summer and raining. I hear the water hitting the skylight over my head, sometimes gently, sometimes hard. The mist is hanging low, obscuring the mountain beyond my window. The leaves of the western maple in the yard glisten. The thoughts and ideas that come to me do not rush by, but arise slowly. I am feeling my way back, not sure of myself.

In the fall of 1925, my father wrote a poem called "Nora."

> *A woman's face young and yet wasted,*
> *By the flames of pleasure and love,*
> *Etched by anguish and furrowed*
> *By the wild impulses of lust.*

Who is Nora? My father does not remember. But he has photographs of some of his friends. "Maybe that one," he says, pointing to a dark woman with marcelled hair and a cupid's bow mouth. She wears lace, presses her hands together with outstretched fingers and holds them to one side of her face. A stylized presentation, not a candid shot. The poem ends with the lines, "And over these features lies a gleam / Of faded beauty, a weary smile which I love." If the lady in the photograph is Nora, there is no hint of the weary smile my father loved. In front of the camera, she is clearly intent on being taken seriously.

Some of my father's phrases sound so young – "etched by anguish," "furrowed by lust." He was nineteen then, less than half my age now. It is strange to feel more mature than my father.

My father reads the poems to me in German and I write them into my notebook with its hard blue cloth cover. Later, my father and I translate the poems. But the rhythm is changed and the rhymes disappear.

I have always read German literature in translation, never in the original. I fear I may be missing something now – resonance and echo. Perhaps there are associations that are lost on me. I think if only I comprehended my father's language more deeply, I would understand him better. My father also feels distanced from himself. He speaks of the young Walter Hans Wiener in the third person. He says, "The man who wrote those poems wanted everything so quiet and beautiful." At twenty-three, he composed this:

> *Oh would that I could grasp the distance*
> *With both hands and leave everything dark*
> *In a wide sea of light.*

There is nothing historical or political in the poems. I know from my reading that in July of 1927, during a violent demonstration in Vienna, the Austrian police killed eighty men. Historians consider it a watershed in Austrian history, an important contribution to the civil war of 1934 and the Nazis' assassination of Chancellor Engelbert Dollfuss. But my father did not directly mark these events. In August 1927, these lines:

I live lost in dreams
And see pictures that emit no light.
I hear sounds foreign to the ears.
And reality is to me the strangest dream.

By 1936, Hitler had occupied the Rhineland. Of this there is not a word. In May 1937, my father wrote,

Tender things growing out of the deep earth
Wish to flower and ripen.

The poems carry few autobiographical details. Sometimes a place is mentioned: Vienna, or Judenburg. With the exception of Nora, no one is named. In December 1937, when he was thirty-one, my father wrote,

Calm breathing by my side,
Night stretches out endlessly.
Outside the window lives the Föhn.
Yesterday has slid away,
Tomorrow nears with light steps.
Quietly I say a "Thou."

But to whom did he speak?

My father has Parkinson's disease now and walks cautiously, as if he does not quite trust his legs. Sometimes I notice a slight tremor in his hands as he holds the poems. He likes me to fetch the dictionary we use and to replace it on the shelf when we are done. He complains often of fatigue. But while we work, his voice is stronger, his expression more animated than usual. He is not so full of passion now. But I am glad that he was once.

After March 1938, the poems stop for nine years.

"Confusing and menacing times," says my father. "Crazy times. Above all, there was the uncertainty. When you came home, you always wondered whether you would find all your things on the sidewalk. Would an SS officer be waiting for you? People were arrested left and right."

My father tells me stories. He met a young woman, Lilly Stifft. She was married but not happily. She invited my father to visit her apartment. When they went in, my father saw a huge portrait of Hitler. "You see — those are the friends of my husband," said Lilly. He was an SS officer. "Can you imagine what would have happened to me if her husband had found me there?" asks my father. We look at each other but say nothing.

My father had a job tutoring the son of a Mr. Fiala who owned the Manner chocolate factory. The company still exists. I know one of their products, thin wafers interleaved with hazelnut cream. I haven't had one for years, but as my father speaks, I remember the taste and texture.

Being Aryan was a condition for filling the teaching position. My father took it anyway. With his blond hair and blue eyes, he did not look Jewish. One evening he was having dinner with the family and a guest asked him when his unit would be leaving. "My kind of people," says my father to me, "were not going anywhere." He told the guest that he had not yet received his orders.

In the university was a barbershop my father patronized. Although it was off-limits to Jews, my father ignored the rule because the shop, which catered to students, was cheap. One day while he was having his hair cut, a man walked in with a white poodle on whose back he had painted a swastika. The barber and the man then had a heated discussion about whether this was an appropriate place for the revered symbol to appear.

I have heard my father tell this story before. But then I did not know what a swastika must have meant to him. Now he smiles as he repeats the anecdote. Did he smile in the barber shop? Did he think, "If this weren't so horrible, it would be funny?"

"What did they decide?" I ask.

My father does not know. "I left rather quickly."

During the early days of Anschluss, some opposition was still expressed. Anti-fascist graffiti regularly appeared on the streets. The Nazis rounded up Jewish people to remove these slogans, and one day a man my father knew was seized. He was a lawyer who also taught at the university. A client of his came upon him. "Herr Professor," she said to him, "do it this way." She took the brush from him and demonstrated how scrubbing with a circular motion was more efficient than using a horizontal stroke. "It will come off so much better like this," she instructed. "What happened to the professor?" I ask. My father does not know.

"Were you ever stopped on the street?" I ask. "No," my father says. "Touch wood." And I notice with interest that he uses the present tense.

I write to my uncle asking him what he remembers about these events. He recounts, "My brother and me wrote many, many letters to people in the United States to many different cities who had the same name like us, Wiener. You wouldn't believe how many American citizens are named Wiener. We wrote them we only need their help for a Visa, but otherwise wouldn't bother them. Not one answered our letters." When I show my father this letter, he says, "We were running around like chickens without heads."

At the time, Jews in Austria faced two problems. The first was obtaining permission to leave, which chiefly involved proving that they did not owe the state any taxes. For my father, this was not so hard. His teaching jobs brought in so little money that he was never required to pay income tax. "I did not give them the satisfaction," he recalls. But the second problem, finding a place to go, was overwhelmingly difficult. By 1938, many countries had begun to shut their doors to Jewish refugees. Britain, Palestine and the United States tightened their rules of admission. Argentina, Chile and Uruguay severely restricted the number of Jews who could enter. Mexico would take no more than a hundred a year. My father had no relatives or friends in safe countries, no colleagues abroad who might help, no international connections.

"I don't remember who told me," he says. "We were always talking about how to get out. One day someone would say that Paraguay was giving out visas. The next day, you'd hear about another consulate. So you'd try there."

Often the rumours turned out to be baseless. But then my father learned about the International Settlement of Shanghai. Although physically part of China, it had been a distinct legal entity since the Treaty of Nanking in 1842. In the 1930s, a municipal council made up of five British, five Chinese, two American and two Japanese members administered the settlement. By July 1937, Japan had successfully attacked Shanghai and gained control of the city's Chinese areas. But the International Settlement and the adjoining French Concession were left alone.

The Settlement had always been open to anyone, including Jews. No passport or work permit was needed to enter. Until August 1939, when émigrés were required either to have a contract for a job or four hundred American dollars, Shanghai was unique in the world. The government was laissez faire in the extreme. Since it offered few services to its citizens, one refugee more or less made little difference.

My father borrowed the money for the passage from an

aunt, Ottla Freund, in Prague, and the father of a friend. He packed his suitcase with a few clothes, the diploma for his doctorate of law, some photographs and his notebook of poems. On October 1, 1938, together with his brother, Günther, and his new sister-in-law, Ditta, he travelled by train to Naples and then to Bari on the Adriatic coast. There the three caught the *Captain Rosso* bound for Shanghai.

"How did you feel about leaving?" I ask. My father replies with a story. In his last days in Vienna, he met an old schoolmate of his, Tomandel, who remarked, "Wiener, you have to emigrate, of course. But I envy you. You will see so many interesting places." My father describes these remarks as those of "your typical half-Nazi." He had no desire to see interesting places. He did not see why he should have to go. Vienna — Wien — was in his blood. Even his name was evidence of his family's ties to the city. He did not know what he would find in China or how he would support himself there. He now says the trip was "like a journey to nowhere."

My uncle had written, "I still remember that my parents were standing at the window of our flat and waved at us, when we passed with a taxi on the way to the South Railway station on the way to Italy." He adds, "I was convinced the Germans would leave the old people in peace, but was mistaken."

I can see my grandparents too. My uncle has sent me a photograph of them. "Vienna in March 1939" is written on the back. It is a formal portrait. A stamp identifies the photographer as Rudolf Franzl and gives his address as 186 Mariahilferstrasse. My grandparents have dressed up for the occasion. My grandfather, Rudolf Wiener, is wearing a dark suit, a crisply starched white shirt and a striped tie. My grandmother, Regine Wiener, née Moldau, has chosen a dark dress and a simple strand of pearls for her neck. Her hair is grey by then, shot through with white. She does not smile and neither does my grandfather.

In my mind's eye, this is how they are, framed in the window of their flat, waving. My grandfather a little taller, standing on my grandmother's right just as he does in the photograph. I imagine my grandmother wiping her eyes as the taxi moves out of sight. Then I see the two old people quiet for a time, lost in thought. Their two sons, their only children, gone now.

"Perhaps I should have done more for my parents," my father says. The remark surprises my mother. In the nearly fifty years of their marriage, he has not said that before.

Mein lieber Walter!

Es sind jetzt gerade 4 1/2 Monate her, dass wir
der Abschied genommen haben und für diese lange Zeit haben
erflucht wenig voneinander gehört, zumindest auf direktem We
ch habe Dir einmal nach Colombo geschrieben, habe dann von D
inen Brief aus Aden erhalten, damit war aber die Korrespond
uch schon versiegt. Auf dem Wege über Deine und meine Elter
ann noch aus einem Briefe von Vilos,den ich vor einigen Tag
m, bin ich aber einigermassen über Dich, Günther und seine
formiert und freue mich besonders darüber, dass Du eine Ste
efunden hast. Ich hoffe, dass sie der Anfang zu einer glückl
rriere sein wird und dass Du auf einem anderen Kontinent d
icht, was Dir Europa und insbesondere unser geliebtes Wien
m wir uns nicht lossagen konnten, schuldig geblieben war.
Über meine Schicksale wirst Du auch so halbwegs u
chtet sein. Ich will daher nur in konzentrierter Form meine
bnisseseit Anfang Oktober 1938 schildern. Nach dem Druck, d
n letzten Septembertagen infolge der drohenden Kriegsgefahr
s allen gelastet hatte, atmete man ein wenig auf. Ich bemüh
ich, hauptsächlich gemeinsam mit Rudi Reich, den wie Du Dich
rn kannst, anlässlich meiner Bemühungen während dieser letz
ptembertage, eine Schiffskarte zu bekommen, getroffen hatte,
anzösisches Visum zu bekommen. Die verschiedensten Versuche
n fehl. Inzwischen ging das altgewohnte Leben fort. Wollten
ter nach Wien, wir waren oft im Kaffeehaus, hatten unsere F
d unseren Spass und glaubten, uns über den Ernst der Lage

R—'s letter to Walter Wiener from Paris, 1939

4

No Names, Please

My father and I sporadically transcribe his poems into my
notebook, usually working for no more than an hour at a
time. My father tires so easily. When I have written all of the
poems down, I type them into my computer in German and
finally print them, twenty-eight in all, on thick creamy paper.
My father chooses a title, *Blumen aus dem Wienerwald*
(Flowers from the Vienna Woods). I make a cover and tie the
loose sheets together with a green silk ribbon. It takes me
about a year to do all this. And then I begin wondering what
else I might be able to find from that period of my father's
life.

I am visiting my parents one afternoon and I ask my
father, "Do you have any letters?" I mean old letters from his
Viennese friends or relatives.

"Maybe, a couple," my father replies.

My mother is more positive. "I've never seen any," she says. I am sitting in their sunroom, surrounded on three sides by glass. In one corner is a hanging basket filled with a cascade of pink roses, in the other is a planter bursting with a profusion of fuchsias and geraniums. The black chest where I found my father's poems is here too. My mother and I rummage through its contents – manila envelopes, binders, photo albums. My father leaves us and goes to the bedroom to sleep. I put a bulging orange file folder containing his papers in front of me on a large round white table.

In it are copies of the *China Weekly Review*, an English-language newspaper for which my father worked in the midforties. The folder also contains lists of books about philosophy and economics, notes for lectures my father gave at St. John's University in Shanghai and even exam questions he set his students in the spring and fall terms of 1943. When I find the letters, they seem thin and vulnerable. Written on postage-saving onionskin paper, they take up very little space.

"But on November 10," one letter, dated February 16, 1939, recounts, "fate caught up with me. In the morning, I saw the Hietzinger Synagogue which was burning, then drove down Prince Eugenstrasse, in order to press for my tax clearance papers, found the Palais Rothschild closed, went a few steps towards the city, was seized by a detective, who asked if I were a Jew, and was taken to the police station in Wieden where there were about 150 fellow sufferers. In the evening, we were brought to the Elizabethpromenade.

"After my interrogation by the Gestapo, who were holding their hearings at the Elizabethpromenade (captured Jews were presented to the Commission there for 6 days and nights and most were condemned to Dachau and for them it was anything but comfortable) I was fortunate enough to spend the rest of my captivity in the Elizabethpromenade (Hahngasse) — that is, in police custody, and the police behaved very decently."

The letter, addressed to my father in Shanghai, is from R——, his childhood friend, who had lived a few doors away from him on Hietzinger Hauptstrasse. It takes me a few minutes to realize that he is describing his experiences in Vienna after Kristallnacht, the Night of Broken Glass. Over twenty thousand Jews throughout the German Reich were arrested that night. In Vienna alone, about 6500 Jews were taken into custody; of these, 3700 landed in Dachau. Shops were destroyed, synagogues burned and Jewish men and women murdered.

R—— was assigned the letter Z, which stood for *zurückgestellt*, or "held back." He explained, "Were it not for the worry over our fate, because a final decision had not yet been made about those of us who had been held back, and were it not also for the worry about our families, because we knew what was happening outside, then one could describe imprisonment as outright jolly, because we 127 people who were housed on the second storey of the building entertained ourselves not badly; there were a few real jokesters among us, who contributed a lot to lifting the mood. It was a chequered company from all social classes. There were rabbis, doctors, lawyers, factory directors, businessmen, agents, employees, craftsmen and workers. Even a Jewish forester.

"Lectures were held, we learned English, a chess tournament was arranged, cigarette packages were converted into cards and domino pieces, and a professional handwriting analyst, whose art either astonished or perplexed us, gave us a glance into the future. Unfortunately, most of the others who were seized did not have it nearly so good, because most

found themselves in emergency quarters such as the Sofien-
sälen, the Nordwestbahnhalle, the Riding school on Pramer-
gasse, Karajangasse and so on. They were under the command of the SS and the SA [Sturmabteilung] and were
horribly mistreated."

R— wrote my father from the comparative safety of
Paris. He had a small cheap room on the fourth floor of a
shabby apartment building on Rue Clauzel. When arrested in
Vienna, he had been carrying his passport and a French visa.
It was a great piece of luck. For that reason, he said, "I am
not sitting in Dachau today but rather in Paris, which is more
beautiful by several nuances."

R— had been freed on November 22 after twelve days of
imprisonment. He managed to obtain his tax clearance
papers and caught a plane on November 26, just one day
before his entry permit to France expired. "I flew from
Aspern...leaving the city of my youth and early manhood,
which gave me so many countless kilometres of Buren
sausages (I think you know the count, you always made bets
about it)."

When my father returns from his nap and reads the passage about the sausages, he laughs and shakes his head. "I
don't remember that at all," he says.

I like R— for his cheerful manner and sense of humour.
Like him too for his kindness and sociability. In his five-page
letter he gave my father the news about over sixty individuals. He wrote how amazed he was at what had accumulated in
the four and a half months since he had last seen my father
for one of their customary daily meetings.

He described the complications that many of his Viennese friends and acquaintances had to overcome in order to
stroll the boulevards of Paris. V— brought her ex-husband
out "very skillfully with a Paraguayan visa, ship's ticket and

a transit permit." Another friend, M—, "was mostly on his legs by five in the morning, wrote countless letters, hammered open the doors of several committees, and displayed an activity that astonished me.... It was mainly because of his tireless activity that his wife was able to come in spite of the greatest difficulty."

Most of the refugees R— knew planned to stay in Paris only a short time. They worried that what was happening in Germany would spread. They feared a war or were troubled by "an undefinable uneasiness." They wanted to leave the continent. One family had already gone to Australia, a second had finally received a permit to live in England. Another woman had left for Alexandria. The energetic M— had been unable to work in France and could not extend his permit to stay any longer. He had booked a passage to Shanghai on the *Chenonceaux*.

R— also had news about people back home. For W—, with whom he had often visited the coffee houses during his last days in Vienna, the immediate prospects were bleak. "I have been trying to secure an affidavit for him, so far without any success." The husband of one of R—'s cousins had been sent to Dachau. Although he was later released, another cousin and a friend were still there. "Unfortunately one keeps hearing of casualties in the concentration camps."

"Now, dear Walter," R— concluded, "I close with the hope that I will soon hear something from you. I hope that the luck which apparently has begun to stick to your heels holds. I knock three times on the wood of my small wiggly table, that it will not disappear again."

My father tells me, "I think my friend made it to New York." But later, my uncle will write, "I don't know about his stay in New York." My parents' black trunk contains no other letters from R—. After the war, there was no contact between the two men. Did he really did manage to escape to the United States? Or was he among the refugees caught in Paris? Was he there on June 14, 1940, when General Georg von Küchler marched in and hung a swastika from the top of the Eiffel Tower?

I look for R——'s picture among my father's photographs. I see him together with his sister, my father and another man on a small sailboat on the Danube. My father sits in front of R—— with his eyes closed and his face tilted towards the sun. Like my father, R—— is barechested. He leans back comfortably, squinting a little behind his glasses. His sister sits beside him, smiling. The other man wears a sailor's cap and works the tiller.

I think about searching for my father's friend. At first, I wonder if there would be any point. He might have died long ago. And if he were still alive, he would be eighty-six. He might not be able or willing to correspond with me. Nevertheless, I decide to try. In the West Vancouver Memorial Library are four New York phone directories, one for each of the boroughs. Densely printed, they contain thousands and thousands of names. I open the directories for Manhattan, the Bronx and Staten Island. No one there has the same surname as my father's friend. In Queens, however, I see that one person does. His first name is different, but I send him a letter anyway. I explain that I have started a book about my family. "I do not know if you can help me. But I am writing on the chance that you can."

A month later, in my mailbox, I find an envelope with an American return address in the upper left-hand corner. But the sender's first name is not that of the person to whom I wrote. I tear open the envelope. The letter is from R——.

"Dear Mrs. Cornwall: When the widow of my cousin returned from her vacation, she found in her mail collected by the post office, your letter, dated Aug. 22. She forwarded the letter to me."

I sit down on the sofa in the living room. I look at the letter again. It seems so improbable that I should be holding this piece of white paper, that I should be reading this small clear script. I feel happy. Happy that R— is alive. And happy that I am able to restore something to my father. Later, he writes to R—, "It is indeed a strange event, that our paths should cross after so many years, perhaps, however, an even greater wonder, that we could escape the satanic plot."

In a separate note to R—, I explain that I have some questions about Vienna, and I also ask for his permission to quote from the letter he wrote to my father so many years ago. I do not have to wait long for his reply.

"It became general knowledge that one could enter Shanghai without any difficulty. A lot of people jumped into this breach and so did Walter and Günther Wiener....I remember darkly that I saw them to the train that started their journey – or was it some other similar event? My memory!

"I, not as active as your father, waited for a U.S.A. immigration visa. Finally, I decided it was necessary to get out too and attained a French visa....After a long waiting period, I got the U.S.A. visa and arrived in New York in February, 1940....You mentioned a letter I wrote to your father from Paris....You have my permission to quote from my letter, it will be an honor for me, but please, no names. Also please keep the letter."

Of course, I comply with this request. I take out all the names. I wonder why my father's friend wishes this. Is there someone he too has not told?

*Walter
Wiener,
Shanghai,
late 1938 or
early 1939*

5

Love Is So Far Away

The letter that R— had written from Paris was typed. Although his sentences were sometimes long, they were easy to read. But I also find two other letters in the orange folder that are handwritten and much harder to understand.

My mother offers to help. She reads the letters aloud to me in German and I write down what she says in my notebook. We puzzle again and again over some of the difficult words. I regret losing even a scrap of meaning. But a few phrases remain indecipherable.

The letters are from my grandmother, Regine. She sent them from Vienna to Shanghai. The first is dated January 23, 1939. "Dearest Walter," she began, in an angular hand not unlike my father's, "we were waiting with great longing for your dear letter, which finally came on Saturday, January 21, this time very quickly, arriving after 12 days. We were very pleasantly surprised by the news, especially concerning your new position, and wish that good luck continues to hover over you. The situation here has become very unfavourable. All Jewish businesses had to be closed, and were Aryanized. As regards myself, so far, I earn enough to make a living and you don't have to worry about us yet. Aunt Ottla wrote that she has not received a letter to date. Write them in detail, it would make her happy. Be sure also to write once to Uncle Viktor.

"As far as our life is concerned, we have already found a basement room because Jews can no longer rent apartments. Dear Walter, write to Frau Kopewitz, we are very dependent on these people."

I know that just before my father left Vienna, his parents had been notified that a German lieutenant wanted their apartment. "I was able to get the eviction order postponed by appealing to a judge," my father says to me. "I told him that my parents were making arrangements to emigrate. When I went, I felt they had somewhere to stay at least." From my grandmother's letter, however, I see that my father's efforts managed to secure their place only for a couple of months.

"We wish you luck in your new position," my grand-mother continued, "and may your many trials not have been in vain. We are both healthy and it is also our only wish to see you once more. Write to us in detail about how you are eating, something that worries us greatly, so that you don't become sick, also how the climate is now."

She finished by expressing her hope to hear from Gün-ther and sent "heartfelt greetings and kisses."

The other letter is dated April 24, 1940. War had begun. The Germans had taken Poland and Denmark. Their con-quest of Norway was almost complete. And by now, Jews from Vienna were being deported to the east.

"Finally, after 4 months," my grandmother wrote, "I received a letter from you and am very happy to have news from you. Dearest Walter, the question of my emigration seems very hazy to me. Father has been in the hospital for seven months and now I have a great deal to do because I am alone. From Bohemia they have written one card in three months. These people really have no interest. [She was referring here to relatives who lived near Prague; among them were Ottla and Alfred Freund, as well as Viktor and Oskar Wiener.] You are very much in error when you think that I could travel to Bohemia. Aunt Ottla and Uncle Alfred have not asked even once what I will do.

"Dear Walter, I just want to see you once more and then God can do with me what he likes. In the house where I now live is a family named Lowitt. Their son has been a choirmaster in Shanghai for six months; he has given concerts there. This man might visit you; because I had no news from you, I asked the man to write to his son. Perhaps this man can help Günther. A sister of his is an actress and they have already performed theatre in Shanghai. Maybe Günther could introduce himself to this family, they are very distinguished people.

"Dear Walter, my longing to see you two is terrible. I don't know how it will end. It is very hard with Father's sickness. He will never be completely well again; he went through dreadful things, two operations, and he can't even sit in bed and is extremely weak. I am with him daily. You can imagine what it means for me, always the groaning; he has terrible pains, gets a daily injection and so it's been for seven months. It would already be enough for me; my nerves are completely shot. The doctors don't tell me much about how Father is. The only answer I get is, one must be patient, he will get better. Dear Walter, perhaps you could write to

Prague after all to see whether I could travel there with
Father. You could write that Father and I can't stand the climate. Perhaps in Prague they could put forward a claim for
us.

"Please, dear Walter, write to Prague, Zirkov Kollarov
9....They might like to take steps for us and find out whether
it is at all possible. I want to work, after all, I can still work, I
don't want to be a burden on anyone."

She then inquired after Günther and his wife, Ditta, who
was not well. She wished her a quick recovery and had a
request.

"So, dearest Walter, one more favour: perhaps you could
send me a little tea for Father so that I could take it to him in
hospital; perhaps that is possible. Ask about it."

Sitting in my parents' house with the sun streaming in
around me, I feel how extraordinary it is that these letters
should have survived. Transported by train across Siberia and
probably by sea from Dairen, a port on the Yellow Sea, they
were delivered to my father in Shanghai. Although he moved
several times while living there, the letters stayed with him.
The war came, the Japanese occupation, a revolution, and
finally another transcontinental voyage, this time across the
Pacific to Vancouver. The letters could so easily have gone
astray. I feel that I have been given a gift.

What about my father? He reads the letters too. But he
does not say anything. He folds them up and puts them back
in the orange folder. I do not ask him what he thinks. Later I
will regret this. But then later I will see what I am doing
quite differently, and different questions will occur to me.

At home, about a month after finding the letters, I translate them into English. I use my dictionary when I am unsure
of the appropriate word or phrase. Gradually I transform my
grandmother's message into a language she never spoke. As I

do this, I realize how quickly she must have written the letters. Sometimes she left out words; some of her sentences were badly phrased. The awkward language makes her distress all the more obvious. My eyes fill with tears. How strange, I think, that I did not cry while the words were German. Although I can read German reasonably well, it is evidently easier for me to feel in English. The tears spill onto my IBM keyboard and run over the grey plastic surface stained by coffee and my children's crayons. I am crying, but I do not sob. I do not make a sound. My chest does not heave. I think of my grandmother, of how alone she was. She asked for so little – a letter to be written, a packet of tea, not even for herself.

I am alone in the house. My children are with a babysitter, my husband at work. I do not feel like phoning anyone. "Dearest Grandmother," I type. "Your sons are now old men. You would probably find it hard to believe that your dear Walter, my father, will celebrate his eighty-fifth birthday in four days. I have two children myself and I am always astonished at how quickly they grow.

"My father is in reasonably good health, although he complains about being tired. You were worried about whether he was eating well, but I think you can rest your mind on that score. My mother is an excellent cook. She has even learned to adapt her recipes to the fact that my father has mild diabetes and should not eat sugar. For his birthday, she will bake him a special chocolate cake using artificial sugar.

"I think you would be pleased to know that you have three grandchildren and five great-grandchildren! My two are a boy, Thomas, nearly six, and a girl, Natalia (we usually call her Talia), who is almost four. People say that Thomas looks much like my father. He is blond and has blue eyes. In fact, it was this family resemblance that prompted me to write to Uncle Günther. I wondered whether he had any pictures of my father as a young boy. We didn't have any, you see, in our photo albums. My uncle sent me a photograph. There were three people in it — my father, Anna Döltl, your maid, and you. In a note, Uncle Günther wrote me that you had died in a concentration camp. I had never been told this.

"As you can imagine, it was a great shock. But I am glad that I know. It helps me to understand my father better. I am grateful, too, that I found out while he is still alive, so that we can talk about it.

"I have read two letters you sent to my father in Shanghai. I can see from them how much you loved both of your sons. In February 1937, my father wrote a poem. In it are the lines, 'All around is darkness, death and the grave / Oh, love is so far away.' So it may have seemed to you too in your last days in Vienna and then in eastern Europe where you died. But I hope it would comfort you to know how well your love has endured. Your dearest Walter was a kind and loving father and I, in turn, love my children dearly. They make me happy. When they are older I will talk to them about you and the legacy of love. With heartfelt greetings, Your granddaughter, Claudia."

I am not sure why I write this letter. In a sense it is useless, because it cannot change how my grandmother died and how she suffered. The words float. My grandmother will never receive them. And although I know all this the tears stop.

When my uncle returned to Vienna in 1949, a Jewish association informed him that his parents had been deported in 1942 to Minsk, in Russia, where they died. Rudolf and Regine Wiener, both. My mother's belief that Rudolf had died before the war was mistaken.

Burg, Rügen Island, August 1937

Look What They Are Giving Me

"My dear Mrs. Cornwall," it begins. "Your letter of June 22 was addressed to my 92-year-old mother at her nursing home. It was just passed on to me since I am the self-appointed genealogist of our family. Since Frensdorffs seem to be at a premium, I am not surprised to find that we are related: your great-great-grandfather, Hirsch Frensdorff of Hamburg, the father of Eduard, was the brother of my great-grandfather, Jakob Frensdorff of Hanover." The letter is from Karl Frensdorff, who identifies himself as "your third cousin once removed."

Some time before, I had written to someone called A. Frensdorff in New York. I didn't know this person; I didn't even know if we were related. I had found the name and the address in the Manhattan phone book after my mother mentioned that there were relatives in New York. I wondered whether I could learn more about her family from them.

Karl includes a copy of the family tree. I see that it starts with Rabbi Meyer Frensdorff, my great-great-great-great-grandfather, who supposedly came from the village of Frensdorf in southern Germany and moved north to Hamburg. His son Michael, also a rabbi, went to Hanover, where he died in 1810. Although it turns out that Karl has never met any members of our branch of the family, my grandfather, Willy, his brothers, Helmut and Arthur, and his sister, Clara, are on the tree. I am pleased to have this family history and interested to know that Frensdorffs had been living in Germany since the middle of the eighteenth century.

When I show my mother Karl's letter, she remembers something that happened in 1935. "It was after the Nuremberg Laws were passed in September. Someone got a copy of the family tree. I don't think it was as elaborate as the one Karl gave you. I don't know who the person was. Or where the family tree came from. But whoever it was gave a copy to Franz Stapelfeldt, the general director at the Ag. Weser shipyard. The intent was to let him know that my father was Jewish."

But Stapelfeldt didn't react the way he was supposed to. Instead, he called Willy Frensdorff to his office. "Look what people are giving me," he said, showing my grandfather the piece of paper on which the genealogy was written. "I wish I had a family tree like that."

"Strange man," says my mother now. "For him to have said that when so many Germans didn't want to have a Jewish background. But he himself came from simple people. Probably no one had ever looked into his ancestors. He thought it was wonderful to know... in modern terms, we'd say, 'your roots.' I never saw the piece of paper," my mother explains. "I don't think Stapelfeldt gave it to my father. Maybe he put it in a file someplace. Maybe he tore it up."

So Willy continued at the shipyard. He had much to do. That year, the Ag. Weser delivered two large ships to the German shipping line Norddeutscher Lloyd: the *Gneisenau* and the *Scharnhorst*. (This was not the battleship *Scharnhorst*, famous for being torpedoed in a spectacular naval battle in 1943, but a passenger ship with the same name.)

Every morning, as he always had done, my grandfather would get on streetcar Number 3 and travel to the east end of Bremen, to the docks by the Weser River.

He was lucky that he could hold onto his job. In *The Rise and Fall of the Third Reich*, author William Shirer writes that "by the summer of 1936, the Jews had been excluded either by law or by Nazi terror – the latter often preceded the former – from public and private employment to such an extent that at least one half of them were without means of livelihood."

Despite this troubling situation, the Frensdorffs felt reasonably secure. In 1933, they had been confident enough about the future to move from the place they rented on Isarstrasse to a house they purchased a few blocks away on Delmestrasse. They did take one precaution, however. Willy legally transferred all his assets to his wife, Melly. The house was in her name, not his.

In our photo album from 1936, the pictures are all very small: five centimetres square. But they are clear, well focussed and bright. Taken mostly by Willy, they show the family on holidays. The Frensdorffs visit Bodethal at Easter, Luhe at Whitsun and Hildesheim in the summer. There is nothing unusual about the destinations. But I find that in itself remarkable, considering the dates of these trips.

In the spring of 1937, the Frensdorffs decided to build a

new house on Weyerbergstrasse in a fashionable suburb of Bremen, Schwachhausen. The house was not large, because Willy wanted to be able to live there when he retired. But it was detached, and it had a bigger garden than the property on Delmestrasse.

Melly was in her element that spring. Her father, Joseph Marholz, had been a general contractor, and she was very happy drawing up the plans and thinking about the look and layout of the house. Sometimes she took my mother out of school to help her make decisions. "We must have done a good job, because when it was done, the contractor asked us if he could copy the design," my mother remarks. The roof went up on April 30, and as was customary on an occasion like this, there was a party, with beer and sausages for all the workmen.

In August, Willy Frensdorff took his summer holidays as usual. This time the family went to the island of Rügen on Germany's northeastern coast. A photo shows Willy on a bridge in Göhren, sitting on wooden steps in the sunshine beside my grandmother. She is smiling, her hands clasped around her knees. Willy is looking out to sea, smoking a pipe.

In another picture identified as *"Brandung"* (surf), my mother, seventeen years old, wades into foaming water, laughing. At Burg, the family visited a beach furnished with comfortable wicker chairs. Flags — including one large German flag with a swastika in the middle — flapped gaily in the breeze. A photograph shows my grandmother buried in white sand up to her neck. She is grinning. Beside her lies my mother. Her head is completely covered in sand, but her torso is exposed. Her left arm cradles my grandmother's head. Willy Frensdorff labelled the picture *"Mann ohne Kopf"* (Man without a Head).

"I wasn't worried," my mother says. "My father wasn't Jewish. He'd left all that behind."

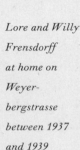

Lore and Willy Frensdorff at home on Weyerbergstrasse between 1937 and 1939

If This Man Dies...

"Why are you here?" my acquaintance asks.

"I was invited," I reply. This is true. But it is not a complete explanation.

We are sitting side by side on a brown polished wooden bench in Vancouver's Beth Israel Synagogue. We are waiting for a ceremony and lecture commemorating the Kristallnacht pogrom that took place on November 10, 1938. A printed program gives the title of tonight's address: "When Light Pierced the Darkness: Christian Rescue of Jews in Nazi-Occupied Europe." On the yellow paper, in the middle, is a picture of a burning synagogue.

My acquaintance is a slim blonde woman in her fifties who speaks with a slight English accent.

"Many of the people here are second-generation survivors," she tells me. "Others feel they must come."

It is the first time I have been in a synagogue. Coming here made me feel apprehensive. The heavy rain, the dark November night, the picture on the program contributed to my uneasiness. But the busyness in the room — people waving at friends, searching for seats — is somehow reassuring. Seven hundred people are assembled this evening, including British Columbia's premier, Mike Harcourt, and Vancouver's deputy mayor, Libby Davies.

"I lost my parents," my acquaintance explains. "It gets more difficult each year."

This would be a natural place in the conversation to say that my paternal grandparents died in the Holocaust. I could also tell her what happened to my maternal grandfather on Kristallnacht. But I nod sympathetically and say nothing.

"Too complicated" is the phrase that goes through my mind. But I know that it is really not so complicated. A sentence or two would suffice to convey the essential information. But I am uncomfortable talking about it, even here, even where I am assured of a compassionate hearing. The conversation moves on to less consequential subjects.

Later, driving home, with my thoughts full of the lecture, I realize that I have behaved with my acquaintance as my parents behaved with me: I have let a moment pass. Perhaps this is why I write the story. Because it is so difficult for me to speak it.

The next day, in a room where the sun is filtered through bamboo leaves, making shadows on the walls and floor, I try to imagine a time more than half a century ago. In my office are two pictures my children have given me. One, done by my daughter when she was four, has an arrangement of large yellow, green, orange and blue blobs. The other, painted by my son when he was five, is of a car, a very square car with six wheels. The body is blue and brown, the hood yellow. You can see the engine, represented by multicoloured dots. The paintings somehow make me feel safe, safe enough to deal with the themes of rejection and hate. Here at home, I am able to write down what my mother remembers of Kristallnacht.

It was either the seventh or the eighth of November, 1938. "If this man dies, then – good night," my grandfather said to his family. Willy Frensdorff was talking about Ernst vom Rath, a consular official in Paris. Herschel Grünspan, a seventeen-year-old Polish immigrant, had shot and badly wounded vom Rath on November 7. Grünspan's father had been among the ten thousand Polish Jews recently expelled from Germany. The young man wanted revenge.

"They were waiting for my father when he came home from the test run of a new boat," my mother had told me. "I remember two sets of *Scheinwerfer*." Quite uncharacteristically, she had lapsed into German. "Headlights" is what she meant. The beams shone through the two shuttered windows that faced onto Weyerbergstrasse, illuminating the walls of the family living room. For a moment, the harsh light played over an old oil painting of a donkey that my mother's grandfather had owned.

"My father was driven back from the docks in a company car because it was so late. He always was, after a test run," my mother recalled. So, first his lights and then, seconds later, the others.

There were two men. They followed Willy Frensdorff down the walk and up the short flight of stairs to the front door. He asked them if he could change his coat. They consented, and my grandfather went upstairs to get out his old coat. No sense in taking a new one where he was going. Meanwhile, the men searched the house.

One of the orders they were following that night was to

"disarm all Jews." A German historian, Regina Bruss, has commented on the irony of that command in her book *Die Juden unter dem Nationalsozialismus* (The Jews under National Socialism). It wasn't as if "generally all Jews ran around armed," she writes. But my grandfather actually possessed a pistol. "I remember when he bought it," my mother told me. "Now I can protect us," he had said to his wife and daughter. In fact, he did not use the gun that night. However, the two visitors found it in a night table next to his bed upstairs and thus picked up a bit of incriminating evidence.

I want to know the exact date that my grandfather was taken away. Was it the tenth? The eleventh? Some Jews, after all, were arrested in the week following Kristallnacht. "What difference does it make in the scheme of things?" my mother asks when I phone her. I am not sure, but I still want to know. I want to know what my grandfather's experience was like. What did he see on his last day of work? What did he think about? What did he read in the paper as he gulped down his morning coffee?

My mother remembers that her family subscribed to the *Bremer Nachrichten*. When I tell her that I would be interested in reading some back issues, she offers to phone Bremen for me to see how I may obtain them. After discovering that the *Nachrichten* is still publishing, she calls the paper, but a receptionist tells her that she should contact the Staatsarchiv (State Archives) in Bremen for any really old material. At the Staatsarchiv, Frau Dorothea Breitenfeldt explains that while most issues from the thirties are available, they must be requested in writing.

Accordingly, I send her a letter asking for copies of the paper from the ninth, tenth and eleventh of November, 1938. I say that I am doing research for a book about my family. About ten days later, a thick brown envelope sits in my mailbox. I open it and see that everything I wanted is there. Amazingly enough, it all survived the heavy bombing of Bremen during the Second World War. I see that along with the copies of the newspaper is a booklet about Kristallnacht in Bremen called "Wir Schritten durch eine Schweigende Stadt" (We Walked through a Silent Town). Although I did not say anything about the pogrom in my letter, Dorothea Breitenfeldt must have guessed that this is my interest.

The newspaper has been reduced to sheets seven and a half by eleven and a half inches. The old German typeface frustrates me: the letter *s* looks like an *f*, *k* like an *r*. I use a magnifying glass.

What surprises me is that on November 9, the top story is not about the shooting of vom Rath. Instead, the lead item is headlined, "The legacy of the dead of November 9, 1923, is realized!" I have no idea what dead are meant. The dateline is Munich, November 8.

The report follows two subheads: "The Führer's festive hour with the faithful at a historic roll call in the Bürgerbräukeller" and "Triumph of belief." The faithful, who are also called "the old guard" and "the comrades," are remembering November 9 fifteen years before, when Hitler led three thousand storm troopers out of this same Bürgerbräukeller in an attempt at a putsch in Munich. It failed, and in the ensuing gunfire in front of the Feldherrnhalle, sixteen party members were killed. These "martyrs who sacrificed their lives" are the dead mentioned in the headline. The newspaper story says that the men who took part in the attempted putsch sit this night "in modest brown shirts." They wear no "insignia of rank," only a red ribbon, "the visible sign of their manly sortie of that time. Today they are not district leaders, officers, ministers, not block wardens. They are what they always were and always wanted to be: the Führer's political soldiers."

I had no idea that November 9 was already such a significant day in Nazi hagiology. I read on. The rooms and gal-
leries of the beer hall are "packed full right up to the last
rafters." At 8:25, someone called Grimminger carries "the
holy sign of the blood flag into the hall and quietly the men
rise up and greet it with raised hands....The tension reaches
its zenith. Everyone has risen from their place; the men stand
on chairs and benches. The Badenweiler March rises to a
crescendo. One only hears the first measures; the following
sounds are drowned out by a storm of jubilation. The Führer
has entered the hall. In the middle of the rows of fighters, a
small aisle opens up for the Führer. Behind him the brown
wave closes in."

The story carries no by-line. However, as I laboriously
translate the German, I think about the person whose words
these were. I use my dictionary a lot. I check meanings. I
want to create the right mood. It is a strange exercise. My
effort to be accurate feels almost like respect. I am extending
the writer the courtesy of being heard. But at the same time
I wonder if I should. After all, it is not likely that he or she
would have extended the same courtesy to me.

At the bottom of the first page is the report about vom
Rath. Dr. Magnus and Dr. Brandt, whom Hitler had dispatched to Paris, issue a communiqué. Vom Rath's condition
has not improved and serious concerns remain. His temperature is still high and his blood pressure is beginning to weak-
en. I leaf through the paper. On page 2 is a poem, "In front of
the Feldherrnhalle — you died and gave us blood so that Germany would awake." I see the weather report — rain and a little cooler. There is an excerpt from a novel entitled *A Small
Woman with Great Courage*. My mother says, "There was
always a novel. I used to read it first." I wonder if she read it
first on this day, too, but she does not remember.

There's a half-page ad for Atikah cigarettes: "Always leads to the discovery of new unsuspected subtleties in aroma…really good cigarettes." Verdi's opera, *Macbeth*, is being performed in the State Theatre. What was the performance like? Gustav Kobbe's *Complete Opera Book* says that the last act opens with a group of Scottish refugees, among them Macduff, singing of Macbeth's reign of terror in Scotland. How did that play in Germany in 1938?

In Bremen, Kristallnacht got underway early in the morning on November 10. Five Jews, three men and two women, were shot, but that day's edition of the paper carries no news of these events. I learn about them from the booklet that Dorothea Breitenfeldt sent me.

The newspaper's top story is about another commemorative occasion in Munich, a restaging of the march to the Feldherrnhalle. "As always Julius Streicher strides at the head, after him the blood flag that since November 9, 1923, is the most hallowed sign of National Socialism's readiness to fight." Drumbeats roll. The Führer strides past columns on which sixteen names have been inscribed in gold letters, "the names of the fighters who fell for the freedom and honour of Germany.…A dirge played by the music corps sounds over the festive place. Emotion seizes everyone's hearts. A hushed stillness lies over the wide space." Hitler walks into "an honour temple" and "decorates his dead comrades with the wreath of immortality. He salutes the heroes and holds silent communion with them."

Although the paper does not mention it, after the pomp and ceremony Propaganda Minister Josef Goebbels informed the party leaders who were present that "spontaneous demonstrations" were to be "organized and executed during the night." According to William Shirer's *The Rise and Fall of the Third Reich*, Major Walther Buch noted these remarks in a secret report that came to public knowledge only after the war.

The news of vom Rath's death appears at the bottom of the front page of the November 10 edition. He "died of his serious wounds," says the headline. His parents as well as the attending doctors watched by his deathbed.

The weather forecast is for milder conditions and some fog. *Oil in the Fire*, a comedy by Franz Lehar, has replaced *Macbeth* at the State Theatre. A local department store, Karstadt, invites people to see its display of toys, "Gulliver's Adventure in the Land of the Lilliputians," in their windows on Obernstrasse. At the Apollo Palace is a new film by Alfred Stöcker featuring fairytales "for all Bremer boys and girls."

On November 11, the lead item in the *Nachrichten* concerns vom Rath's funeral in Paris. Readers don't discover until page 5, under the headline "Bremen's revenge for the Jewish murder," that Bremen's synagogue was burned to the ground. The story says, "As in many other towns and cities in the Reich, so in Bremen on Thursday night, the justified indignation of the German people about the cowardly assassination of embassy official vom Rath, instigated by international Jewry, was powerfully expressed....In the early hours of the morning the Jewish temple in the Gartenstrasse burst into flames....The Jews of Bremen were taken into protective custody. In spite of the monstrous rage that was understandably aroused by the death of embassy official vom Rath, all measures against the Jews in Bremen were executed with the highest discipline." Not a word about Dr. Adolf Goldberg and his wife, Martha, Heinrich Rosenblum, Selma Swinitzki or Leopold Sinasohn, the Jews who were killed.

Lehar's *Oil in the Fire* is still being performed at the State Theatre. There's an American film, *Chicago*, starring Tyrone Power and Alice Faye, at the Tivoli. The ad for it shows a woman wearing a corset, long gloves and a big hat, her hands on her hips. The Decla has *Scotland Yard Seizes Hold* and the Metropol is showing *The Experimental Hour*, a movie dealing with "modern problems between husband and wife." In the classifieds, E. Mettcker advertises one thousand Christmas trees and Karstadt announces the sale of game and poultry "ready to cook and roast." From the personals, I learn that the Miessners' "dear little Edith" has left them forever, that the Bartels are celebrating "the lucky birth of a healthy son" and that Isolde Renken and Hans Kaiser have become engaged.

And what of my grandfather? In the back section of the November 11 edition of the paper, on page 20, under "Shipping News," I find a small item that relates directly to one of my questions.

The report says that "the Norddeutscher Lloyd accepted delivery of the ship *Iller* on the 10th of November, 1938, after a successful test run. The vessel was built by the Ag. Weser shipyard."

This was undoubtedly the test run of which my mother spoke. It had been completed by November 10. On that day the *Iller* was back in port and delivered to its new owner. The orders that set Kristallnacht in motion were transmitted sometime during the early morning of the tenth. My grandfather must have been seized that night. While the Gestapo were interrogating my father's friend R— on the Elizabethpromenade in Vienna, they were also taking my grandfather into "protective custody."

I still don't know whether the *Iller*'s test run was a one- or a two-day affair. I don't know when Willy left to go on it. On November 9, when everything still looked normal? When did he see the shattered glass and read signs such as "Revenge for the murder of vom Rath" for the first time? Where was he taken after his arrest? By reading the booklet from the Staatsarchiv I learn that on November 10 a group of Jewish men and boys were taken from Bremen to the Obslebhausen prison. On the following day, they were sent to Sachsen-hausen, a concentration camp north of Berlin. I wonder if that is also where my grandfather went.

"I don't remember being told where my father was sent," says my mother when I ask. And she is not certain now which camp it was. "But we must have known, because we sent him letters. I remember writing him that 'What doesn't kill you will only make you stronger.' I think it's a quote from Nietz-sche. It was Sturm und Drang time. An eighteen-year-old will write that to her father in a concentration camp."

One day in December 1938, my mother answered the door and there was her father. He came in, covered his shaved head with his hands and wept. "I had never seen him cry before," says my mother. She covers her own head as she tells the story.

My mother and grandmother and grandfather celebrat-ed. They bought Pomeranian goose breast for themselves and, for their cat, Schneeman, a hunk of lean hamburger meat.

"I think Franz Stapelfeldt intervened for my father," says my mother.

"Do you know what he did?"

"Maybe he said he needed him at the shipyard." And then my mother remembers something else about Stapel-feldt. "He continued to pay my father's salary, even after Kristallnacht, when he couldn't work at the Ag. Weser any more. A courier delivered it to our house."

Now I am really curious about this man who was my grandfather's boss. Why was he so different from the people around him? And how did he manage to get Willy Frensdorff out of the concentration camp? To whom did he speak or write? Did he assist other people too?

Again I write to Dorothea Breitenfeldt in Bremen. I ask whether she has any letters or documents that would show what Franz Stapelfeldt did for my grandfather. I also ask her whether she knows where my grandfather was imprisoned. If I can get this information, I reason, I may be able to find documents concerning his release in the camp's archives.

A few weeks later, Dorothea Breitenfeldt replies that she is not able to tell me where Willy Frensdorff was taken in November 1938. But she does have some relevant information: a letter from my grandfather to his former boss.

"Dear Mr. Stapelfeldt," Willy Frensdorff wrote, "I will never forget how completely generous you were with me and my family in our most difficult times. I have you and you alone to thank for the fact that I was freed from the concentration camp in good time. You did this for me without thinking of the danger that it put you in with respect to the Nazis."

The letter confirms that my grandfather was rescued. But still I am not satisfied. The details are missing, and I am determined to ferret them out.

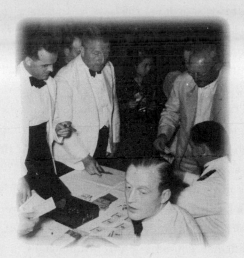

Willy
Frensdorff
on board the
Scharnhorst,
July 1939

Waiting and Waiting Again

Willy Frensdorff's datebook for 1939 is the size of a pocket-book and covered in soft dark leather. The words "*Deshimag Bremen*" and a triangle containing the letters "*AGW*" are embossed in gold on the outside. Inside, the first few pages are taken up with photographs of ships — the *Oslofjord*, the *Unitas*, the destroyer *Paul Jacobi* and the submarine *U 29*, all built at the Ag. Weser shipyard.

I knew there were diaries in the black chest in which I had found my father's poems and the letters from his mother. But I had never tried to read them before. They were written in German, of course, and the handwriting was very small. Now my mother reads them to me, sometimes using a magnifying glass.

Jan. 2. Call Regierungsrat Schulz Gestapo. Schulz's phone

number, 21411, is listed at the back of the diary (under *G* for *Gestapo*). I notice that someone else in the Gestapo, Parchmann, can be reached at 21511. However, the name that keeps recurring is Schulz, always with a title attached. Sometimes my grandfather shortens the "Regierungsrat" to "Reg." or "R. R." But even in the privacy of his own diary, he never neglects to include it. No wonder, perhaps, because Erwin Schulz was the chief of the Gestapo in Bremen and had been since May 1934.

I have not learned this from my grandfather's diary, but from a book called *Bremen im Dritten Reich* (Bremen in the Third Reich) by Inge Marssolek and Rene Ott. Dorothea Breitenfeldt had copied a few relevant pages for me after I wrote telling her I was curious about what kind of man Schulz was.

Jan. 3. My grandfather is not thinking about emigration. He wants to stay in Germany and continue to work for the Ag. Weser, as the director of the electrical department. But how? By the end of 1938, Jews are no longer permitted to run businesses, to practise law or medicine. They cannot hold public office or join the civil service. Journalism, radio, farming, teaching, theatre, films and the stock exchanges are closed to them.

My grandfather's younger brother, Helmut, is so depressed by these restrictions that he and his wife turn on the gas in their Berlin apartment. When my grandmother, Melly, receives the news that the couple and their poodle have died, she cries and asks, "And the dog, why did the dog have to go too?"

Still, my grandfather hopes that an exception will be made for him. Perhaps he thinks that the authorities who have permitted him to work this long will wield their influence again. *Discussion with R. R. Schulz. Departments of the*

*navy, defence and Gestapo have nothing against my employ-
ment in building of warships. First let the grass grow over the
past. Take up employment only after my rehabilitation.*

It is hard now to imagine what "rehabilitation" my
grandfather could have expected. Nevertheless, Schulz rec-
ommends that he write to Hermann Göring, minister of the
interior and commander of the Luftwaffe. He advises my
grandfather to be brief and to the point, to emphasize the
favourable opinions of the navy, defence and Gestapo. He
should not expect an answer for four to six weeks.

Jan. 5. Willy Frensdorff takes his letter to the director of
the Ag. Weser, Franz Stapelfeldt, who will deliver it to Herbert Göring, a relative of the better-known Hermann. The
relative, who is on the board of directors at the Ag. Weser, has
agreed to pass on my grandfather's application.

Jan. 9. Messenger brought salary. Although my grandfather is no longer working at the shipyard, Stapelfeldt continues to pay him and will do so for months to come. *Telegram
from Stapelfeldt. Change in my letter to Göring wished.*
Stapelfeldt thinks it wiser for my grandfather not to mention
that he has been involved with building warships. He should
just say that he has been working for the Ag. Weser. *Fourth
page changed and left with Stapelfeldt's girl.*

Jan. 10. Stapelfeldt takes the letter to Herbert Göring in
Berlin.

Jan. 11. Paul, a friend, visits my grandparents and
describes some of the possibilities for my mother in England.
My grandfather writes a birthday letter to Stapelfeldt.

*Jan. 17. Considering whether immigration to Abyssinia is
possible.* One factor in favour of Abyssinia (now Ethiopia) is
that my grandfather speaks Italian. Since Mussolini's inva-
sion in 1936, the country had been an Italian colony.

Jan 19. Ag. Weser is launching a new cruiser. I wonder if

Willy Frensdorff watches the event, or does he just hear about it? On this day, he also records that Siemens Werke, the large electrical machinery company, has agreed to pay the royalties due him as a lump sum of 9000 marks rather than in installments. My grandfather had patented a new method of wiring lights on ships that made maintenance and repair much easier.

Jan. 21. Stapelfeldt will go to a training camp near Munich for two to three weeks. Stapelfeldt spoke yesterday with Herbert who asked if I had received an answer and said there were thousands of similar applications.

Jan. 23. Child is acknowledged as non-Jewish. My grandfather is writing about my mother. According to the Nuremberg Laws passed in 1935, marriage between a "full" German and a "full" Jew was strictly forbidden. If such a marriage took place after 1935, the child would be considered Jewish. But if the marriage had occurred before 1935, the children were not necessarily considered Jewish.

The booklet about Kristallnacht that Dorothea Breitenfeldt sent me contains a reprint of an article from the *Bremer Zeitung* of April 4, 1937 — "Who Can Marry Whom?" An illustration shows circles divided into quarters. Each quarter represents a grandparent. A circle with four white quarters stands for a "full" German, one with four black quarters signifies a "full" Jew. And then there are the circles representing those who fall somewhere in between. Someone with three Jewish grandparents is for all legal purposes Jewish. A person with two Jewish grandparents is a first-grade *Mischling*. Someone with a single Jewish grandparent is a second-grade *Mischling*.

My mother had two Jewish grandparents but she had been baptized as a baby. In 1939, a *Mischling* who had been baptized early in life was treated differently from one who was of Jewish religion. "I could have married a German," my mother tells me, "although the authorities would have had to agree. They probably would have measured my head." (Certain proportions were considered typically Jewish and less desirable.) If she had not been baptized, such a marriage would not have been possible.

Jan. 24. After all, we want to take in hand the preparations for emigration. This represents a change in my grandfather's thinking. He has finally acknowledged that he may not be able to stay in Germany.

Jan. 26. Willy Frensdorff goes to the local police station. He is late complying with a law passed in August 1938 requiring that all Jews take a recognizably Jewish first name. There is, however, no penalty for his tardiness, and his request to become Hans Martin Wilhelm Israel Frensdorff goes without a hitch.

Jan. 27. Consul gives little hope. There are enough Italian engineers.

Jan. 30. My grandfather has passport photographs taken and sends off his 1938 tax declarations. (He cannot leave until all outstanding taxes have been paid.) He reminds himself to buy Baldrian drops, a mild sedative.

Jan. 31. Application to Göring through the Interior Ministry negatively decided. Willy Frensdorff expresses no anger or disappointment. The only other thing he writes down that day is the name of a city, Alexandretta. This is a notoriously unhealthy, fever-ridden town built on a swamp along the south coast of Turkey. But its unique legal status makes it a possible destination. In 1937, because of a dispute between France and Turkey, the League of Nations established Alexandretta as a separate entity controlling its own internal affairs. The situation lasted until June 1939.

Feb. 1. Called English consul. Go to Turkish consul.

Feb. 2. Called Stapelfeldt. Call again when the written refusal is in my hands.

Feb. 3. Call the Italian consul for Abyssinia.... Information about Haiti. Immigration closed.

Feb. 6. Called R. R. Schulz. Stapelfeldt advised against sending letter to Zettlitz Nielsen before the interview with Schulz. First listen to what R. R. Schulz says.

Feb. 7. We ask Ella, a relative, to help us emigrate to São Paulo.

Feb. 8. My grandfather calls Schulz to arrange for another meeting. *Can't this week.* He will phone back on the thirteenth. The English consul, Bullock, is leaving on a three-week trip to England.

Feb. 9. Nothing to remark. Waiting, waiting again and waiting.

Feb. 13. Call R. R. Schulz. The discussion is postponed again.

Feb. 14. Noon discussion with R. R. Schulz. Decision taken....Has no hesitation about giving me a passport. Asks if I had already been to the consulates. The phone numbers for the consular offices are in the back of the diary. I find numbers for the American, Brazilian, British, Chilean, Costa Rican, Cuban, Chinese, Dominican, Ecuadorian, French, Guatemalan, Haitian, Honduran, Italian, Liberian, Mexican, Nicaraguan, Peruvian, Paraguayan, Swiss, Swedish, Siamese, Turkish and Uruguayan consulates. Twenty-four in all. *Should inform Schulz in ten to twelve days and keep him up to date.*

There is something hypnotic about the way my grandfather applies his engineer's mind to the problem of emigration. Methodically he explores one avenue after another, as if he were working out a particularly tricky electrical installation. He never complains or despairs. I say to my mother,

"I think it's amazing that he wasn't angrier."

"I don't think he ever was," she recalls. "I think it tickled him a little to try something else."

I realize that, under the spell of my grandfather's approach, my mother and I are not angry either. We try to understand what he wrote, to fill in the background that is missing. When he mentions that Schulz had no hesitation about giving him a passport, for example, we wonder if he expected to encounter difficulties. Could problems have occurred because he had worked on ships for the military? Might the authorities have insisted he stay because he was privy to confidential information?

We wonder about these things, but we express very little emotion. Only later, when I start writing about this time in Willy Frensdorff's life, will any feelings surface. And then only in a confused way, in a dream that I describe in my diary: "Gordon and I become friends with an Arab. For a while we are friends, and then for some reason he becomes angry with me, says I should go to live in Israel. I am surprised by this. I thought Arabs did not exactly encourage the settlement of Israel. I say, 'But my grandparents' people lived in Germany for three centuries. Why should I leave? This is my *home*. Canada is my *home*.' "

I mix up Canada and Germany. But the feelings are clear: the fear that what happened to my grandfather could also happen to me, the resentment of the possibility. "Why should I leave?" My grandfather never mentions any bitterness. Did he experience it, though?

Feb. 15. French consul general. Brousse, the director of the Society for the Navigation of the Rhine and an engineer for the Georgeline Society for Transatlantic Navigation. To Brousse a letter, ask for help.

Feb. 16. Telephoned the American consul in Bremen.

Philippines here. All other possibilities with the consul general in Hamburg.

Feb. 18. Airmail letter to the High Commissioner of the Philippines in Manila. G.D.S. [Stapelfeldt] *has visit from H.G. and no time.*

Feb. 21. Müller telephoned. China. Will ask Melchior.

Feb. 25. A colleague, Fritz Neef, has another idea. A ship-builder in Abo (now Turku), Finland, not far from Helsinki, might give my grandfather a job. Neef offers to write a letter to a Dr. Tachel in Holland who may be able to make the connection.

Feb. 28. Wrote to the Society for the Protection of Science and Learning in London.

March 1. Made appointment by telephone with the English consulate.

March 3. Answer from Society for Protection of Science and Learning. Answer from Ella. São Paulo. Immigration is closed.

March 4. Willy Frensdorff visits his older brother, Arthur, in Hamburg to discuss working for a firm called Percy and Donald in England and also visits the consuls general of China and Brazil.

March 6. Call R. R. Schultz. Wants a written report about what is undertaken so far.

March 8. Sent telegram to Brousse.

March 9. I.D. card, photo, police. G.D.S. no time….A solution will probably emerge.

March 10. Wrote to B. Valensky in England.

March 12. Wrote to M. de la Grange in France.

March 14. Koster telephoned. Is going to intercede for me in South America. My grandfather does not describe these plans in detail. But for some reason they involve posting a letter to Koster's aunt in Natal, South Africa.

March 15. Wrote to the International Committee for the

Placement of Intellectual Refugees. I know from my reading that German troops poured into Czechoslovakia that morning. In the evening Hitler made a triumphant entry into Prague.

March 18. The English consul, Bullock, is back from England but sick.

March 21. Afternoon to the English consul.

March 23. Central Trust of Shanghai written by air.

March 25. Wrote to the Committee of Friends in London and International Committee Geneva.

March 27. Telephone Guatemalan consul.

March 31. Call Glässel. Ernst Glässel is on the board of directors of the shipping line Norddeutscher Lloyd and is an Ag. Weser shareholder. He also founded his own company with interests in Asia. *Looking for engineer in Siam.*

April 13. Brazilian consul. My grandfather learns that a visa is issued only to those persons who have permission from the Brazilian government to settle and buy land. Paraguay? There's a closure on immigration, but the consul is going to inquire about it.

April 14. Consul for Siam. It is possible to stay for thirty days if one has enough money. *I told Glässel that, in any case, I have decided to settle in Siam with my brother.*

April 17. Parchmann. Papers for emigration.

April 19. Tax office Bremen.

April 21. Foreign Exchange Office. Police Room Number 123.

April 23. Discussion in Hamburg. Finally Shanghai. My grandfather has discovered that Shanghai is the only place in the world that does not require a visa to land. In April of 1939, the city does not restrict immigration in any way.

When my father arrived in Shanghai from Vienna in October 1938, a few hundred Jewish refugees were living there. By the time Willy Frensdorff made up his mind to go, thousands more had come. Indeed, it was such a popular destination that it was difficult to buy tickets for the passage. Later my grandfather would write in a letter to Stapelfeldt, "It was due to Director Hashagen that I could book the trip out on the *Scharnhorst*, the last ship with emigration possibilities for me and the family of my brother's. Without his help, it wouldn't have worked."

Hinrich Hashagen was the head of the nautical/technical department at Norddeutscher Lloyd. My grandfather had met him through work: the German shipping line was one of the Ag. Weser's best customers.

On July 10, Willy Frensdorff shared a glass of schnapps with Franz Kruppenbacher, another engineer at Ag. Weser. He sent letters of farewell to a couple of friends and to his sister, Clara, in Hamburg. The next day, he steamed out of Bremen on board the *Scharnhorst*, the comfortable cruise ship built four years previously by the Ag. Weser shipyard. My grandfather had designed the electrical installations himself.

My grandmother, Melly, and my mother, Lore, accompanied my grandfather as far as Genoa. His brother Arthur, sister-in-law Thea and nephew Hans Joachim were also on board, bound for Shanghai. Melly and Lore planned to wait in Germany until Willy could support them in Shanghai. In the meantime, they would live on money from the Ag. Weser. Stapelfeldt had promised that until Willy had a new position, his salary would be paid to Melly.

Arthur was able to bring his family with him because he had money waiting for him in China. Like other refugees, he was restricted by the German policy that permitted each emigrant to take no more than ten marks out of the country. This wasn't much money. It had about the same purchasing power that fifty Canadian dollars have today. However, Arthur had a benefactor.

My mother tells me that someone in New York transferred money to Shanghai for Arthur. She does not know this person's name. When I contact her cousin, Hans Joachim Frensdorff, who now lives in Hamburg, he remembers the man as "Mr. Badenhop, a business relation of my father's." But neither my mother nor her cousin know any details about the arrangement. They don't know whether the money was a gift or a loan, or whether it was intended as the start of a business venture. They also disagree about the sum involved. My mother thinks it was about $10,000 U.S.; her cousin believes that it was closer to $2000.

Naturally, I am curious about Mr. Badenhop. I read through my grandfather's diary again to see whether I might have missed a reference to him. Eventually I find one buried in some notes at the back where my grandfather kept a list of letters he had written. I see that one went to "Badenhop – New York." But Willy recorded no first name and no address. I write to four Badenhops listed in the New York phone directory. I receive a couple of replies, but the letter writers know nothing about the Frensdorffs. Later, I will write to several archives about this man, but nothing ever turns up.

At the back of my grandfather's diary, I find his careful notes about the price of the fare. He bought tickets for himself, Arthur, Thea and Hans Joachim. The total cost was 6425.70 marks, a sum that represented nearly half of his yearly salary of 14,000 marks. The plan was that once Arthur arrived in China he would repay Willy with the money that Mr. Badenhop had provided. This would give Willy enough to live on until he could find a new job.

As the *Scharnhorst* cruised into the Mediterranean, the Frensdorffs saw the sights along the way. They stopped in

Barcelona, snapping a picture of five Spanish soldiers leaning on their rifles in front of a brick wall. They visited the botanical gardens and a cathedral. In Genoa, they rode in an open carriage. My mother sat beside the driver, who wore a bowler hat.

After leaving the *Scharnhorst* in Italy, my mother and grandmother returned to Bremen by train. My grandfather spent several more weeks at sea: Port Said, the Suez Canal, Colombo, Singapore, the China Sea, and finally the Yangtze River. The whole journey took a month. In that time, the open-door policy that had allowed between 15,000 and 18,000 refugees to land in Shanghai since December 1938 had changed. While the *Scharnhorst* was at sea, the Japanese introduced the first of several measures that would make it more difficult for Jews to enter Shanghai. On August 9, they announced that after August 21 they would not permit any additional Jews to live in Hongkew, a district they had controlled since 1937. Impoverished refugees often settled in this poor area because of its low rents. Jews already living there did not have to leave but were required to register with the Japanese authorities. On August 14, the Municipal Council that controlled most of the International Settlement of Shanghai followed the Japanese example. No more refugees would be permitted to live in the Settlement. But my grandfather, his brother, his sister-in-law and his nephew arrived on August 10, just before the new regulations took effect. They could stay.

Hans Joachim, who was four at the time, describes their arrival in a letter to me. "A small jetty takes us from the large SS *Scharnhorst*, lying at anchor in the Yangtze River, to the Bund, that famous road along the embankment. The water is dark; it's late in the evening and ahead I can see the glittering lights of Shanghai."

On September 2, my grandmother wrote, "Dearest Willy: Thank God that it worked to just get out. The *Scharnhorst* was the last ship." The *Scharnhorst* was not in fact the last ship to bring refugees to Shanghai. Boats still on the high seas when the new regulations were established were permitted to land. Some boats scheduled to leave Europe between August 14 and August 21 were also allowed to dock. But it was the last German ship to make the trip. "Ships travelling after the *Scharnhorst* were called back in Rotterdam," my grandmother recounted in her letter. "I just have to imagine this happening to our trip and my hair stands on end."

On August 25, the German government warned its merchant fleet about impending hostilities with England. At dawn on September 1, 1939, German armies crossed the Polish frontier. The Second World War had begun. It was now too dangerous for German passenger ships to venture into the Pacific.

In the months to come, the regulations in Shanghai concerning refugees would be relaxed a little. Persons who could bring $400 U.S. with them or whose immediate family were already in Shanghai would be allowed to enter the city. But only two to three thousand more Jews would settle there.

"Look at this," says my son one afternoon while I am working in my office. He is carrying something he has constructed out of yellow Lego blocks. "It's an airplane," he explains as he makes it swoop through the room and land on my printer. "These are inventors." He points to two Lego men sitting on the wings. "They've just invented a plane to take them to Shanghai because there are no more boats."

*Willy
Frensdorff's
German
passport,
1939*

9

I Cannot Bury the Hope

When Melly and Lore Frensdorff returned to their house on Weyerbergstrasse in late July, they discovered that everyone on the street knew what had happened. "But I don't care," wrote Melly to her husband.

The garden was a profusion of snapdragons, dahlias and gladiolas; the scarlet runner beans had climbed to the upper storey. The sour cherries were ripe and the campanula was blooming for a second time. However, the heat of the summer was gone. "July 25. My dear Daddy: I think everything is weeping for you, because since we've been back in Germany it has been raining almost constantly. Your Lore."

Melly and Lore wrote over a hundred letters to Shanghai. To keep them all in order, my grandfather bought a blue binder for $3.93. He put the letters in the binder as soon as he received them, with the most recent on top.

Half a century later, when my mother and I take the letters out of the black chest, they are still in the same order. We remove them from the binder because we are afraid that the rings, now a little rusty, may tear the fragile onionskin paper. I put the letters into beige legal-sized file folders and carefully label them. My mother and I begin to work through the letters. She reads them aloud and I record her doing so. Eventually we will fill eighty hours' worth of tapes.

"July 27. Dearest Willy: I sometimes think that it is all a dream.... We no longer feel really at home here. I would never have believed that I could separate myself from everything without regret. Your Melly."

"July 28. My dear Daddy: Hallelujah! This morning there was a letter from you! We must have read it at least a dozen times because it is a little as though you were here yourself." When Lore learned that Willy had lost his favourite pen, she immediately dispatched another one by airmail. "It is waiting for you in Hong Kong. So don't be sad any more. Your Lore."

The two women began to clean the house. Systematically, they cleared out cupboards and chests. Their tidying often made them think of the absent Willy. All over the house they found notes that my grandfather had written to himself in his small neat hand. "Bring in the peas. Twine against the sparrows. Pansies. Gladiolas." Meanwhile, Willy Frensdorff had started to look for a job in Shanghai. *August 12. Called Hohn. Is away, back next week.*

On August 19, my mother painted a sketch of herself washing and polishing her father's car. In the picture, she wears tall black boots, blue shorts and a chartreuse blouse. A green scarf almost covers her red hair. She holds a red hose in her right hand and at her feet are flowers. She labelled the picture, "*Dein wild west Mädel*" (Your wild west girl). She wrote about her plan to go to Vienna in September and study at the Michelburen School of Fashion. She would live with Melly Frensdorff's stepmother, Hedwig Marholz.

"Should Gramma bake poppy-seed and nut cakes? You would get them by airmail," Lore wrote. Melly approved of this idea. She added a note to the letter, "The idea of [sending] Viennese cakes and strudels is very good, only a war better not get in the way. It would fit badly into our program.... The situation is very tense."

But, of course, the outbreak of war did interfere with the sending of nut cakes and much, much else. "Sept. 2. My dear Daddy: Since yesterday, the German troops have been advancing. The air force has the order not to drop bombs on open cities or on the population but only to attack military targets, and the enemy fliers should do the same. However, if they fail to conduct war in a humane fashion, Germany won't either. Your Lore."

My information about Willy's introduction to China comes largely from his diary. He kept copies of a couple of the letters he wrote then (also in the binder), but the bulk of his correspondence is lost. I piece things together by interweaving notes from Willy's datebook and passages from the letters he received. The effect is slightly odd. Sometimes it seems as if Willy, Melly and Lore are talking at each other.

Sept. 7. Made appointment with Hohn in two weeks.

"Sept. 8. Dearest Willy: I just heard the Führer's talk. One should be able to conclude that the war is now at an end, because absolutely no demands are being made of the western powers and the Treaty of Versailles is finished. Love, Melly."

On September 15, the German trains that had temporarily reduced their service were running normally again. My mother's school in Vienna announced that it would offer instruction despite the outbreak of hostilities. In Shanghai, my grandfather made his first diary entry in English. *We looked new apartment Avenue Pétain.*

On September 17, my mother travelled to Vienna and moved into her grandmother's apartment on Berggasse. School began the next day. My mother was lucky to be a student. Otherwise, she would have been taken by the Weibliche Arbeitsdienst (Women's Labour Service) on September 21 for an unspecified term of duty.

"Monday, Sept. 24. Dearest Willy: The Polish campaign has ended in the astonishingly short time of 18 days. Normally that is the same time that a letter sent [to Shanghai] via Siberia needs for its trip.... Dear Willy, a thousand times a day I think that everything is here, house and homeland.... I don't give up the hope that if, with God's help, we now achieve a lasting peace with disarmament, then the Jewish problem will finally be cleaned up and our daddy can come back to his small house."

"How could she think that?" I ask my mother as we read the letter together.

"She still didn't consider that my father was Jewish," my mother says.

I shake my head. It is hard to understand my grandmother's hope, her belief that there might yet be a place for Willy Frensdorff in Hitler's Germany. Even harder to comprehend how she could link his return to the "cleaning up of the Jewish problem."

On October 2, Melly was distressed to learn that Willy was considering cashing in his return ticket to Bremen. "I don't see why that's necessary," she wrote. "But I suppose, if one day I had to pay for your return fare, I could sell Fahrenhorst [a property in the country] and the car."

"When your father left, did he intend to come back?" I ask my mother.

"I'm sure he didn't," she said. "He knew that was it. But he was probably required to buy a return fare along with the passage out. Then, because of the war, you couldn't take a ship from Shanghai to Bremen. Maybe that's why he could get his money back."

Oct. 5. Phoned Hohn twice.

Oct. 11. Application sent to Shanghai Power Company.

"Oct. 11. Dearest Willy: The times are exceedingly revolutionary. Just think, all pooches must be inspected to find out whether they would be useful in the military service. Many will have to part from their loved ones. On my way home from Gosslar, a lady sat across from me with an Airedale terrier on her lap. I asked if he also had to go away, and she said, 'Luckily he looks so bad that he is unlikely to be taken!' "

But Melly Frensdorff also alluded to more serious matters. "Naturally you don't have the slightest idea what is going on again. Soon I won't either. In the meantime, Lore visited me again for a few days. We had to discuss something that we couldn't settle in writing. When you read the enclosed copy, you will be in the picture." But there is no accompanying letter or note that explains why my mother returned home between October 2 and October 11. All I know from subsequent letters is that her visit was brief, and that she left Bremen in such a hurry that she forgot her nightgown and her leather jacket.

In my mother's next letter to her father, written in Vienna and dated October 17, she imagined herself having conversations with her father or sitting with him beside a warm stove saying nothing. "Have patience, it will come. If three souls are of the same mind, it must become reality." She described how food was being rationed but how she had more than enough bread and meat. She told her father not to worry. "The German flag stands with a watchful eye over

Germany's borders so that not much will get through, and it would be even more difficult for something to cause damage." She also described her classes and complained that her grandmother kept trying to introduce her to eligible young men. "So I said to her, 'Dear Grandmama, I won't find a man like my father.'" But there is nothing in the letter about what took her back to Bremen.

Was it too risky to let the censors see? Is that why the enclosure that should have explained everything was missing? Is that why my grandmother phoned Vienna rather than writing a note?

"You must come home," she said.

"Do I have to?" my mother had asked.

"You can't get out of it."

The Gestapo wanted to see her. She wasn't told why. She recalls double doors and a staircase. My grandmother, who had come with her, waited at the bottom while my mother walked up one flight. She found "a very empty room. Two guys in there." One of the men showed her a gun. "Do you recognize this?" he asked. "It was my father's," she told him.

My mother's memory of the rest of the interview is hazier. "There was something about the car. Someone had seen me driving it."

"What shall we do with her?" asked one of the men. "Might as well let her go," said the other.

"I was probably naive," my mother says now. "I was not afraid."

Perhaps she does not remember the fear. She tells me that when she visited Bremen with my father she tried to find the old Gestapo building. She remembered the street, Am Wall, but not the number. Walking up and down, she said to my father, "It must have been near here." But the buildings looked different and she couldn't find it.

I remember when my parents took that trip, about fifteen years ago. I recall my mother telling me afterwards about my father's impressions of the city, which he had never seen. "It reminds me of Salzburg," he had said. "It's so small and charming. Everything is within walking distance." My mother told me about looking for her old high school, Oberlyzeum Kippenberg. But she had not mentioned searching for the Gestapo offices.

"Oct. 14. Dearest Willy: I just walked through the garden at twilight. The last dahlias are frozen but this year we have so many beautiful winter asters and your carnations are still flowering in front. Otherwise it is very fall-like. The stove is on, very cosy. I never see why our daddy can't be here. It wouldn't cost a penny more or trouble anyone. As I have often written to you, I cannot and will not bury the hope that everything will return to rights. I am constantly assailed, partly on the phone, partly on the street in town, for news of your welfare." Melly told Willy that many people, including Margaret Luer, his secretary at the Ag. Weser, sent their greetings. A friend of my mother's, Evi Jahn, had promised to write. "All say, 'Perhaps Herr Frensdorff will return soon after all.' How we all like to hear that!"

Oct. 19. Interview at the Shanghai Power Company. Will get more information from Head Office. Nanking Road.

"Oct. 22. Dearest Willy: Why must there be a war again in Europe since one knows from the outset that it doesn't solve any problems, only makes them more difficult? The Tommies, after all, are also risking their necks, and what will they do with us 80 million people if they do win? In the west [of Germany], nothing is happening, in the east [Poland], it's over. We are turning our attention more to the North Sea. This famous U-boat that snuck into Scapa Flow, torpedoed two of their newest ships and came out whole has given the whole Navy a lift. Now stare astonished into the ether, Mr. Churchill! Where is the *Royal Oak?* Where is the *Repulse?* 'We are sailing, we are sailing against England.' It's become a hit, this forgotten song from the world war by Hermann Loens. Your Melly."

Since Willy had arrived in Shanghai, he had been pursuing a position with Theodor Hohn at the China Company. Unfortunately the man was elusive, making appointments and then postponing them. Scribbled in the back of my grandfather's diary are the names of other businesses: Jardine Matheson and Co., Shanghai Docking and Engineering Co., Szechwan Power Project. But his attempts to contact them seem to have yielded nothing.

However, on October 27, Willy went for his second interview at the Shanghai Power Company. He wrote a lengthy letter about it and kept a copy in the binder with all the other letters. Moving from his terse datebook prose to this is like stretching. I feel a sense of relief. Maybe Willy did too.

"My dear Melly and dear Lore: I was taken to Mr. Perrin. Very elegantly appointed private office. Mr. Perrin, a typical older dried-out American, very polite and obliging, asked me to take a place opposite him at his large diplomat's desk. Mr. Perrin remarked upon my age and said that his company didn't like to employ men over forty, and further, that my last job was more in the field of ship electronics. I replied that age offered a good guarantee of extensive experience and that I, as my references indicated, had much to offer in the field of the transmission of electricity.

"Then Mr. Perrin opened the salary question and asked what I wanted to earn. I said to him that I was not certain about salaries in Shanghai, but that I would probably need between $300 and $400 to support myself. I asked him to tell me what payment was usual and let him know I wouldn't make my acceptance of a position dependent on the question of a salary. Perhaps you will wonder why I have become somewhat timid about the question of a salary. But it is understandable. It is hard on one's nerves to come so close to getting a position and then see it founder on the demand for pay.

"In addition, I cannot keep it a secret any longer that the relationship between me and Arthur has unfortunately become so unbearable that I must strive with all means to make myself independent." My grandfather didn't explain what the problem was, although he mentioned a "heartless" contract that Arthur had given him to sign. "My only real contact is with Thea, with whom I can speak my mind from time to time. She suffers as much as I do from Arthur's nervousness."

"Oct. 30. Dearest Flower," Melly wrote to Lore, who then forwarded the letter to her father in Shanghai. "Last night I had an unusual gruesome dream. I was going home in the pitch-black darkness. Suddenly a lighted skeleton with a grinning skull appeared in front of me. Not so pleasant. Your Mamitschka."

In Shanghai, Willy was waiting for an answer from the Power Company. Apparently Mr. Perrin could not make a final decision without the approval of his boss, Director Howkins. And Howkins was in Japan.

"Nov. 6. My dear Papalino: I showed your splendid photographs around the class. The girls were all enthusiastic; many would also like to have such a daddy in Shanghai. If they only knew...here naturally no one knows anything and you are there on a long business trip. Your Lore."

On November 10, Howkins returned from his trip, and Willy went twice to the company headquarters on Nanking Road to find out whether he had a job. During his second call, he was given an employment contract to sign.

It took nearly a month before the good news reached Europe. When the letter arrived, my grandmother was with her cleaning lady, Frau Ella Bösking. Both of them jumped up with excitement. "If you want to see a happy person, then look at me!" Melly shouted. Frau Bösking cried a little and wiped her eyes. Melly immediately wrote to Lore in Vienna, telling her all this. In her rush, she forgot to date the letter. "My good Lofrechen: Oh, child, for a long time there has not been such a happy day. Our daddy is unique and shining. Like a sleepwalker or dowser in quite strange circumstances he has found the water channel in our desert. 'Delight' is not the word for it. I feel tremendously blessed that he understood how to free himself from such chains....The word will immediately go around properly, and so it should. I would like to hold it under the noses of a certain group of people, to show them what they have achieved with their meanness. Just the opposite of what they wanted! Your happy writer."

Both my grandmother and my mother were quick with their congratulations. "Dec. 9. Dearest Willy: That is a great thing you have succeeded in. I don't need to tell you how boundlessly happy I am. I think I am the happiest I have been in my whole life....It won't be long until the last few years will disappear and fade. You will become completely young again....By the way, Nov. 10 is an especially fateful day for us. Nov. 10, 1912, was our wedding day; on Nov. 10, 1918, you came home from the war; last year on Nov. 10 was the catastrophe, and now on Nov. 10 your rebirth. Out of pure joy, I brought Schneeman a true quarter pound of genuine lean minced beefsteak....I see our daddy at the wheel of a car again, speeding down Nanking Road in a large open Packard! Your Melly."

"Dec. 12. Dearest golden Daddy: I can't sleep from pure happiness that you are freed from all of your shackles, can work again, earn foreign currency....It is as if this curtain that darkened our whole horizon for so long has been lifted and one sees behind it a sunny landscape! And we wanted to creep to Fahrenhorst to hibernate. Instead of that a new large life begins – it goes around in my brain like a kaleidoscope and I am supposed to sleep! Never mind, I take it gladly; happy things hover in front of me. I would have liked to see you when you came home with the employment contract. I would have liked to see Thea and Arthur too. Did you order a nice bottle of champagne, or what did you do instead? When fewer letters come, we will know that once again you are working from morning till night to earn dollars. Boy, Dollar-Prince, how we envy you!"

Nearly two weeks later, on Christmas Eve, 1939, my mother was typing a letter to her father. This was very unusual for her, since up until then she had written to him by hand, in green ink. She and her mother had been feasting as much as the wartime shortages allowed. They had eaten chocolate, marzipan, raisins, dates and five walnuts each. They had drunk a glass of schnapps but missed the cup of coffee that traditionally followed Christmas dinner. The previous day, my grandmother had received thirty-three whole coffee beans as a present. But she had brewed them three times and the scant tablespoon of coffee would yield no more.

At half past twelve, my mother was still feeling a little peckish. Some undefined Chinese delicacy would be just right, she thought, but she settled for a bit of cheese and sausage. "It's a funny Christmas," she wrote to her father. "Next year will be more splendid." They would be in their bungalow in Shanghai, her father wearing a tuxedo, she and her mother in long evening dresses. As my mother worked, my grandmother brought in a green bean salad. "It tastes wonderful!" my mother typed. "Do you know what made us quite crazy? That you are picked up and brought home in a car. That is much more fabulous than at the Weser,,,, Mommy immediately told everyone, 'My husband already has a car again, moreover a large Packard.' I would have said 'a gilded Rolls Royce,'" joked my mother.

Franz Stapelfeldt wrote too. "It made me very happy to hear that in a relatively short time, you succeeded in finding a position that suits your talents." After that, he stopped paying my grandfather's salary.

"You never asked why your grandfather went to Shanghai," my mother says to me after we read these letters from December of 1939. She is right. Although I always knew he lived there, I never wondered why. And now my lack of curiosity puzzles me. At the age of fifty-seven – not normally a time for seeking adventure – Willy Frensdorff had left his job and his country, his continent, in fact. He went at a time when his skills in the shipping industry were much in demand. The Germans were rebuilding their navy and the Ag. Weser was humming with activity. But I hadn't thought his trip required a special explanation. Part of the reason surely lay in the fact that my grandfather was working in Shanghai. If he hadn't been, I suppose I would have wondered what impelled him to go, to give up everything.

Among some notes at the back of Willy Frensdorff's diary I find the draft of a letter. I do not know for whom my grandfather intended it. He writes in English, "Obeying this suggestion from the General Consul of China I apply to your company. I beg you to instantly help me leave [the word *escape* is struck through] this country and I will never forget the service you will in this way render me [*and my family* is crossed out here]. In respect to the urgency of my application I should be very obliged to you if you" – there the draft stops.

The pictures of my grandfather's travels were part of my

childhood. I had pored over them many times, but never with an appreciation of the urgency that lay behind these images. Now I return to our family photo albums, wondering if there are clues I failed to notice. Was I missing something?

"August 1939, Daddy Trip Out, *Sharnhorst*," my mother has written beside some of these pictures. I see my grandfather sitting in a wooden deck chair, wearing a peaked cap, a double-breasted jacket and light flannel pants. He looks away from the camera. My grandmother is next to him reading a book. Then I see my mother in a two-piece swimsuit, carrying a bathing cap, evidently on her way to the pool.

I look at my grandfather again, standing at a gaming table wearing a white suit, money in his right hand, his eyes upon the table. Beside him are other men wearing white jackets and black bow ties. They wear their hair short and slicked back. In the lamplight, their heads gleam. One man holds a cigar. My grandfather does not look like a man who is escaping something. His face does not betray the mixture of relief and apprehension that he probably felt.

Later, in Shanghai, fifty-seven men and one woman gaze at a camera from a lawn in front of a low building. They are arranged in three rows; the first row sits on chairs, the second and third stand. About two thirds of the people are Caucasian, the others Chinese. They all wear Western suits. And, despite the sunshine, many of the men have vests as well as jackets. The collar on the woman's jacket is fur. This is the Shanghai Power Company. My grandfather is in the second row, smoking a pipe.

In another picture, Willy Frensdorff is lying in long grass, propped up on one elbow, smiling a little. In the background are tall leafy trees. A page marked "Prosper Paris Road, 1940" shows my grandfather wearing light-coloured shorts and a short-sleeved shirt. He is sitting on a stool using a telephone. Beside the phone are tulips. A grass mat covers the wooden floor. A small watercolour of Moses being rescued from the reeds hangs on the wall. I know the painting well, because it hangs now on my own bedroom wall. My grandmother must have bought it. On the back, above the artist's name, she signed hers with a date – 1935.

And from the same period, my grandmother's stepbrother, Kurt Marholz, in his Wehrmacht uniform with the eagle emblem on his right chest. He is seated at a sun-dappled table under a tree, eating pineapple out of a tin. On the table is a notebook, its pages fluttering in the breeze, and a pen with a bottle of ink. Could I have seen anything in these images? Would someone else have?

What if I had seen that other picture, kept not with the photo albums but in the black chest? My grandfather looks straight at the camera and does not smile. He wears glasses, a dark suit, a striped tie and a white handkerchief in his pocket. This is the photograph signed "Israel Willy Frensdorff." It's on the second page of his passport. On the top of the first page is printed "Deutsches Reich," and underneath that is an eagle holding a swastika in its claws. Beside the eagle is a large red *J*, three centimetres high. When I first found this document, it seemed to radiate. I felt that if I passed my hand over it, I would find it immediately even if my eyes were closed.

Now it seems strange to think of it lying there all along, within easy reach.

Melly and Lore Frensdorff
in Germany, 1936 or 1937

10
___

As in a Dream

By early January, 1940, my mother was back in Vienna. The
winter that year was cold. Lore Frensdorff walked the streets
of the old imperial city muffled in a sheepskin coat with a
kerchief wrapped tightly around her head. It snowed cease-
lessly; the tiny flakes seemed like "many many small, wonderfully pretty, good luck stars — more than enough for the
three of us," she wrote to her father. One afternoon, she
ordered an azalea for her mother's birthday at a florist on
Opernring. It was at least -14° C. On either side of the street,
the drifts were nearly a metre high, blown by the wind into
crazy comical shapes "like white sand dunes." People wore
colourful woollen hats and scarves, and many used their skis.
St. Stephan's Cathedral in the centre of the city was completely snowed in. My mother bought chestnuts at a stand

near the graveyard and for twenty *Groschen* (pennies) warmed her hands and stomach.

In Bremen, the temperature did not rise above -10° C for weeks. When her coal supplies dwindled, my grandmother heated only the kitchen and used it as her living room. She moved a round table into the middle of the room, brought in some wicker chairs and a lamp. For additional fuel, she sawed up an old white desk that had belonged to her Aunt Eda. "Perhaps she is turning in her grave," she wrote to my mother.

But the two women did not complain about the cold or the shortages because they did not expect to spend another winter in Europe. They were planning to join Willy in the summer, after Lore obtained her Master's papers.

"Jan. 19. My dear good birthday Mommy: On your next birthday my Chinese boy can hand you a branch of cherry blossoms early in the morning. Daddy, a complete gentleman with his nice white hair, and his elegant daughter in an embroidered Chinese dress can congratulate you. Your Lofre Lörchen Rosamündchen."

"Jan. 27. My dear good Dollar Daddy: Mommy wrote me in her latest letter, 'I wish you could wind up things at school soon and we could go.' It must be a nice feeling for you to know that we are not coming just out of decency, but that we are tremendously happy. For us, and especially for me, it is far better than if we had dozed away our entire lives in Bremen. For today, bye from your fashionable sparrow."

Thinking ahead to my grandfather's birthday in March, my grandmother wrote this: "Jan. 31. Dearest Willy: In all the long years, there was not one hour of material deprivation. Tirelessly and patiently, you provided everything necessary for a splendid existence, and once again you have achieved the same with the fullest success. It is actually everything that one can require of a mortal.

"So with the deepest gratitude for what you have done until now and will continue to do, I give you my solemn promise that in the Far East I will replace your expensive homeland as well as I can. It is no small task, but with our courageous sparrow beside us, we will get everything. Everything is going along well. Perhaps this letter will arrive just in time for your birthday. I will buy a bouquet of tulips as always but all three of us will have to forgo the Dobostorte that we used to have. Now butter cream is tasted only in our memory.

"With sunshine in one's heart, there is nothing difficult any more. Think now how nice it will be when Lorinchen begins to earn and takes on some of your burden. Mommy always had it the easiest of us three and soon I won't have anything to do any more but radiate goodness and warmth like a stove.... Good and loving wishes, Melly."

By February, my mother's reasons for staying in Vienna began to seem less compelling. "Feb. 25. My dear Mommy: What do you say to setting off on our trip immediately? I will go without my Master's papers. In the end, what is important is that I know something and not that I know what is required here.... Just think what is at stake if one day we can't travel at all. Perhaps we will also get the last train as Daddy got the last ship.... Your Lorli."

"Feb. 29. Dearest Willy: It seems to me that fate requires us to be totally unmaterialistic. I am ready for it. Maybe completely new experiences will open up for us. In general, one must forget every fear; maybe that is the secret of the greatest success. Melly."

German passenger ships had not travelled to Shanghai since August 1939. It was still possible to sail from Italy on the Lloyd Triestino line, but another route, which involved taking the Siberian Express through Russia, turned out to be cheaper and safer. Melly and Lore decided to go by train to Moscow, where they could board the Siberian Express for Harbin in Manchuria. There they would change trains and travel to Dairen, on the Yellow Sea. From Dairen, they could catch a Japanese ship, sail south for a few days and finally dock in Shanghai.

The details of the trip were complicated, the paperwork daunting. Melly and Lore needed new passports and visas for many countries: Lithuania, Latvia, Russia, Manchuria, Japan and China. (The Japanese visa was required because Japan controlled Manchuria.) Landing or entry permits for Shanghai were also necessary because of the new regulations that had been introduced eight months before. Fortunately, since my grandfather's position with the Shanghai Power Company was secure, there was no trouble about obtaining them.

My grandmother needed to prove that she had remitted all outstanding taxes. "It will be necessary to pay an additional 3500 marks. I will have to sell the car and [the property at] Fahrenhorst," she explained to Willy on March 19.

German currency restrictions determined how much cash Melly and Lore could take with them and how much of the journey they could prepay from Germany. For the entire ten-thousand-kilometre trip, Melly and Lore Frensdorff were allowed only ten marks in cash each. They had to leave the rest of their money in Germany. They were allowed to pay for the train trip as far as Harbin, but my grandfather had to pay for the balance of the journey by transferring Japanese yen to Manchuria.

The regulations about the transportation of household effects changed every few weeks. On March 14, my grandmother had written that she could use German money to pay for the transportation of their furniture as far as Vladivostok. On March 27, it seemed that marks could pay for the shipping of the household goods only as far as the German border. On April 15, it appeared that they could travel as far as Harbin for marks, provided that the appropriate transit permits had been obtained.

"I feel guilty when I read this," says my mother. She pauses a moment, and my tape recorder makes a faint whirring sound as the tape continues to go round and round. "How could we be so concerned about our furniture? When you think about the worries other people had."

The letters do not mention those other people. I ask whether this was because all the letters had to pass through the hands of the censor. Or was it because my mother and grandmother did not know what was happening? Because they did not allow themselves to know?

"We had no Jewish friends," my mother remarks, trying to explain. She looks out at the patio. The clematis vines that trail along the eaves of the house are dripping with pink blossoms. "We didn't know anyone who was taken away. Clara [Willy's sister, who lived in Hamburg] was still there. The problems weren't vivid to us; we didn't talk about them. We talked about the war."

"April 15. My dear good Daddy: What do you say to the slap that the English received? I believe that the Führer just waited for them to make such a mess. They laid the mines themselves that closed the entrance to the Norwegian harbour, probably wanted to spare us a little work. Daddy, if you could have experienced it. One evening we heard that the English were laying mines in Norwegian territorial waters and the Germans couldn't do anything. Then the same night we marched into Denmark and Norway. The next day we were occupying the capital. One can only say that the Führer is a master at exploiting the opportune moment. As we heard the special broadcast, I was completely wild with joy. Your Lore."

"Was I German, then?" asks my mother. She raises her eyebrows, shrugs. "When did I change?"

Even my grandfather, Willy, still seemed to be rooting for the Axis side. On April 19, he wrote to Melly, "Congratulations to the new soldier!" He was referring to Kurt Marholz, my grandmother's stepbrother, who was at this time laying communication cables in preparation for the assault on Belgium.

Towards the end of April, my grandmother rented the house on Weyerbergstrasse to an officer in the Luftwaffe on the condition that he take care of her cat. She kept the garage to store her furniture, because she had determined that to move it would be too complicated and costly. "We will find an inexpensive Chinese [worker] to make us some affordable furnishings – even if they are only made out of packing case wood. Today our happiness does not depend on such things," she wrote to Willy.

In May, after Melly obtained the visas she needed, she discovered that another recommendation from the Ministry of the Exterior was required as well. "No one knows what's what; everything is constantly changing....I guess you are waiting impatiently for news of our departure, but you couldn't be more impatient than we are ourselves. Your Melly."

My grandmother and my mother left from the main railway station in Bremen on May 25. They travelled for over two weeks. In Russia, people smiled at them and gave them potatoes. In northern Manchuria, they saw camels walking in the distant hills. They ran out of money in Harbin and did not know where to spend the night until they met a Japanese man who spoke some German. He noticed a notebook of my mother's that the German electrical company A.E.G. had given to her father. The Japanese man said, "Oh, you are A.E.G? I am A.E.G. too! Come stay with me."

Telling me this, my mother laughs. "The Japanese fellow showed us into his living room and indicated that we could rest on a couple of rattan chairs. I think my mother didn't sleep a wink; she kept worrying about whether he had designs on me. But he was just being kind."

My grandfather noted in his diary that Melly and Lore arrived on June 14. However, he said nothing about the reunion, about how he felt when he saw his wife and daughter walking down the gangplank from their ship, the *Tsingtao Maru*. He did not mention that he had made a reservation in the Palace Hotel for a couple of days to make their introduction to China more comfortable. He did not record their reactions to being in Shanghai.

Twenty-year-old Lore found the International Settlement full of novelties. People from all over had come to the crowded port by the Whangpoo: Sikhs, Scots, Englishmen, Americans, exiled Russians, Frenchmen, Poles. It was worlds away from homogeneous Bremen. Lore discovered a Chinese vegetable market selling produce that she had never seen and could not identify. At the German butcher, Fütterers, she bought roast beef, rare and thinly sliced, as well as blood sausage and salami. In the Café Federal on Bubbling Well Road, she sampled Swiss pastries: cream puffs and almond crescents, fruit tarts and napoleons. She ate lunch in the Chocolate Shop with its red lacquer façade, its white-uniformed Chinese waiters and its soda fountain. There she tasted banana splits and ice cream sundaes for the first time. Her clothes were all wrong, but she didn't care. Soon she found a fabric store, La Donna, on Nanking Road, bought herself an Italian cotton printed with leaves and made herself a new dress.

But Melly hated Shanghai. She hated the crush of people and the smells. She hated picking her way through the beggars who sat on the sidewalks and pleaded for money with outstretched hands. She felt claustrophic in the place Willy was subletting on Seymour Road. It had high ceilings and two large windows overlooking a lane, but it was a single, sparsely furnished room. There was only one table holding medicine, marmalade, cups. There wasn't even a balcony or a window box for flowers.

"I remember sitting on a bed crying," says my mother.

"Were you mad at her?" I ask.

"No, I must have understood her reasons. Although I'm not sure I do now. She had a choice," muses my mother. "My father didn't." And so, in spite of the war and the uncertain future, Melly chose to go back to Germany, alone.

Willy wrote nothing about her departure, about how he and Lore had accompanied her to the Whangpoo Wharf and waved as her ship sailed north. Picking up the first letter my grandmother wrote as she was travelling back to Germany, my mother reads, "My two dearly beloved: Tomorrow I hope to be able to give up this first little letter — "

"The date?" I ask, interrupting.

"The thirty-first of July," my mother replies. And then, her voice rising with surprise, she asks, "How long did she stay? Just six weeks." My mother had forgotten that the visit was so brief.

Melly was aboard the *Tsingtao Maru*, the same ship on which she and my mother had travelled just weeks earlier. "As in a dream, I wander around this familiar ship — everything like last time. Only eight or nine weeks lie in between and my dear travel commander is not here. How strange it is."

Before sitting down at a desk with her purple pencil and a sheet of the ship's cream and red stationery, my grandmother had eaten lunch. It was soup, baked fish, roast chicken, pineapple with cream, and coffee. She called it "tiffin," an Anglo-Indian expression. There were other Germans aboard. "I sit quietly and peacefully surrounded only by pleasant northern European faces."

Looking up, my mother says, "You see, she struggled so with this. She is so happy she is in — " She breaks off. It occurs to me that my mother is struggling too — to make sense of Melly's attitudes. "She didn't like the Chinese. She talked about *diese schlitz Augen*, these slant-eyes. She said she didn't want to see so many of them. I was different. I took to the Chinese right away. I thought they were wonderful people."

My mother returns to the letter. "The whole morning it was so nicely cool and breezy." The remark reminds her of the way my grandmother suffered from the climate. "And the heat," my mother explains. "She couldn't stand the humidity. She lost weight. We all did at first, my father too. But she was scared she would die in Shanghai."

"With a light chop on the sea," my mother resumes reading, "I sat on deck with lemonade, but at the moment I am sweating a little again. That must and will probably stop in Europe. At noon I thought most affectionately about my Flower sitting with her good daddy in the Chocolate Shop for tiffin, going afterwards in the bus to Bubbling Well and tastefully arranging the place. I am happy that at least I know all your surroundings so well. Now I can be with you in my thoughts day by day and hour by hour.

"I will make myself a chart showing the hours [in Shanghai] so that what I think about you is right. With this parting, one thing became quite clear to me. Our next reunion will be a final one. By that time, everything on our side and on the other will be clarified so that one will be able to make proper long-range plans. I hope with all my heart that in a short time this will be the case. That means that we won't need to be separated for a long time. When the Flower comes running up to me with a fresh happy face...and little Daddy is round and satisfied again, yes, that will be first rate. My beloved two, my only beloved in this world."

"She was a funny lady," comments my mother.

"Do you think she would have stayed if she had arrived in fall, when it was cooler?" I ask.

"I don't think it would have made much difference. It was such a culture shock for her."

Melly was the one grandparent I had known. When I was thirteen, she came to Canada. She stayed with us for a couple of years and then found her own apartment a few blocks away. I remember that when she lived in my parents' house, she was often sad. There were arguments and tears. Melly went for long walks alone. Once on a sunny day she sat in her room for hours wearing dark glasses. The curtains were drawn, the door only slightly ajar. My father said to me, "She is oozing doom."

The image I have of my grandmother on that bright day is still clear. I can see her seated in a high-backed chair behind a coffee table in her dark wood-panelled room. I can even visualize her sunglasses, the way the rims curved slightly upwards to form points. But most of the words, hers, mine and my parents', have vanished. Only my father's comment remains. If I had known about her then what I know now, would I have understood her unhappiness better?

Melly waited for two days in Harbin to make the connection with the Siberian Express. She liked the city, admired its broad streets, lush green gardens and blue-eyed Russians wearing traditional smocks. She described them as "Tolstoy figures." She booked into the Grand Hotel, a comfortable place where the staff spoke German. In the dining room, six canaries flew in and out of a large cage, landing on lamp-shades and plants. Sometimes they sat in a line on top of a large tile stove and sang. They were almost white, their bellies a pale yellow.

Walking on the beach along the Sangara River, Melly found a flower market filled with gladiolas, zinnias and cornflowers. But her thoughts, she wrote to her daughter, were "always and always with you." In her spacious room, hot tears streamed down her face as she recalled the times when Lore would sit and sew and she would sit beside her helping. "These are my fondest and happiest memories."

The train took Melly back past Lake Baikal, grey and stormy. Back to Irkutsk. Back across the Siberian plains, through the endless birch forests. Back to Moscow, where she sat in a café across from the Kremlin under pale blue skies drinking iced coffee. Back to Vilna. Back to Berlin.

On August 18, she wrote, "The situation here is unchanged. One believes that the end will come soon. That would be fortunate for mankind."

Melly decided not to return to Bremen but went instead to Goslar, an old walled town in the Harz Mountains, where she had waited for Willy during the First World War. Here she gained back the weight she had lost in China and on the journey. She wrote that her nerves were much better. She was sleeping as much as twelve hours a night, uninterrupted. She went for long walks by day and by night.

"Oct. 21. Yesterday evening was such beautiful moonlight. I wanted to see Goslar from above in the moonlight and went a short way up to the edge of the forest. Then nearby I heard the call of a rutting stag. Oh, that sounds frightening! I ducked down and waited. Once again I heard the sound. Perhaps an opponent that I couldn't hear answered from somewhere. Then I went home, somewhat relieved when I noticed the game fence nearby. Would the violent one have made a play for me?"

Almost as soon as my grandmother arrived in Germany, she began thinking about returning to China. Had she forgotten how much she had disliked Shanghai? She planned to go the following year, in September, when the worst of the heat was over. She dreamed about seeing her family. "I was reunited with you two in a pleasant dream. I had been away for a long time and you were waiting for me in the Weyerbergstrasse at the front entrance of the house. And Lörchen said, 'Now, Mommy, don't you see anything?' There was the front garden full of zinnias in all colours, lovely beds, a wonderful trimmed lawn and then these calendula tied into large stalks in Lore's esteemed fashion. Colourful marble gravel. Everything perfect and Daddy had his hands in his trouser pockets and grinned with pleasure."

But it was not to be. Melly would never see her Willy again. There would still be letters. They would travel from the Harz Mountains through Siberia to Shanghai until the Russian campaign began in the summer of 1941. Then they would travel across the Atlantic Ocean, over South America and across the Pacific to China. The news, most of it six weeks old, would be read eagerly. The letters would arrive every five to seven days until the Japanese attacked Shanghai in December of 1941. The occupation would slow them down to a trickle – a few sentences every few months, transmitted by the Red Cross.

Willy never lost his affection for his absent wife. For her birthday on January 23, 1941, he wrote, "No evening goes by that I don't say to Lore before going to bed, 'Would that Mommy were here.'"

It is the end of May, 1992, and I have been reading family letters for five months. One night I dream about Melly. I dream that I am sobbing inconsolably because I was not with her when she died. In the dream I had taken her to a hospital. I intended to return later that night, but before I did, she died. I sob and sob, and though I seem to be grieving for my grandmother, I say, "All those lives, all those lives." I dream that Gordon puts his arms around me. But he does not ask me why I cry, and I feel I cannot tell him unless he does. My cheeks are wet with tears, as wet as if I had washed my face. But when I wake, my eyes and cheeks are dry. I have a terrible feeling of loss. I feel regret that I did not know my grandmother better. I think, "I wish that I had known her as the woman crouching down in the moonlight, listening to the call of a stag."

The depth of my feeling surprises me. I didn't weep like that when my grandmother died fourteen years ago. Is it an effect of reading her letters? And why did I dream that I could not talk about my grief until I was asked? Is it because my father did not talk about his loss until I asked? And those lives — all those lives. Whose are they? Why do I cry in my dream but not when I am awake?

*Fashions
for spring,
1941*

Walking Home

The elevator in the building at number 160 on Avenue Edouard VII in Shanghai's International Settlement rose slowly. It was Thursday, March 6, 1941. As the red-haired woman with the widely spaced grey eyes stepped out on her way to the offices of the *China Press*, a Shanghai daily newspaper, the blond blue-eyed man regretted not striking up a conversation.

Normally, he would be getting out too. He was the financial editor of the *China Press* and this was his floor, but that day he had business upstairs. When he finally returned to his office, he broke into a smile as he realized that the woman he had admired in the elevator had come to see him. She sat in front of his desk with a folder containing fashion sketches. Actually, "sketches" is not accurate. The better term is "collages." They were made of black, grey and brown paper cutouts, and they showed the red-haired woman's latest designs.

There was one of a Chinese woman's face in profile. She wore a beret-like hat, high in the front. Another showed a Caucasian woman in a broad-shouldered dress with raglan sleeves and a slim skirt. The top was brown and grey, the skirt brown. On the bottom of each sketch it said, "Modellofre."

Who spoke first? I don't know. But I know the woman's purpose. She wondered if the *China Press* would publish her sketches. Would they be interested in articles on fashion? She mentioned the name of an Austrian couple, friends of her father and apparently also of the financial editor. They had suggested she see him. The editor said he would see what he could do. Where could she be reached? She lived in an apartment on Route Prosper Paris in the French Concession, she said. There was no phone, but he could always leave a message with her father at the Shanghai Power Company.

Two days later, they met again. And then again the next afternoon. Walter Wiener had wondered if Lore Frensdorff might be interested in observing the fashionable ladies who could be seen at the tea dances in the Park Hotel, a handsome art deco building overlooking the race course at the junction of Nanking and Bubbling Well roads.

"April 24, 1941. My truly beloved," my grandmother wrote to her daughter, "how happy I am that everything is so delightful with you, not only materially but also emotionally.... Now this first party, so much fun....And even a cavalier from Vienna on the Danube. With a telephone call and the Park Hotel. And how clever my *Bumsche* is to immediately smell the roast. I'm astonished. It is grand....That must have been awfully interesting. Including *Schlagobers* [Austrian dialect for 'whipping cream'], caviar and Russian black sweet."

My mother is reading the letter to me in her kitchen. We are sitting at a round white table in front of a sliding glass door. Beyond the door, along the white stucco wall of the house, is a brick planter filled with pink geraniums. Inside, on the wall opposite me, are prints of pictures by Gustav Klimt, the Austrian painter who died in 1918. They are square pictures of field flowers, seen from a distance; small yellow, white and pink blossoms float over a green background.

"Dr. Wieland," my mother continues. And then she stops reading to explain. "You see, I didn't tell her his name was 'Wiener' because I was afraid for her. I knew the letter would be read. I didn't want her to have any more trouble. People would recognize 'Wiener' as Jewish. I didn't want them to be asking her all sorts of questions."

She turns back to the letter. "If the chap is as nice as his name then I'll let him please me," Melly said in closing.

Our family photo albums contain pictures of my father on horseback. He wears a checked tweed jacket, a checked ascot and jodhpurs. He's with a friend, an American named Eric Schmidt. They ride beside bamboo fences, dirt roads and water-filled ditches in a district called Hungjao. There's a low building with Chinese characters painted on the façade. The landscape is treeless. To my West Coast eyes, it seems barren. Along the wall of one building are bushes with no leaves. It must be winter.

The horses are small, ponies really. Once a year horses were driven down from Mongolia and sold in fairs as far south as the Yangtze River. They were lively animals, and riding and racing were a central feature of Shanghai's social life.

My father had never ridden in Austria. However, when his new British and American friends invited him to do so, he did not like to admit that he was a novice. On his first time out, he tells me, the horse did not co-operate and kept returning to the stable. In the pictures, my father looks very serious.

My parents went swimming, played tennis and ate chestnut confections in an Italian patisserie in the French Concession. For a summer party, Lore made herself a new floorlength dress. Small blue flowers on white cotton. Short sleeves. A tight waist and yards and yards of material in the skirt. Willy Frensdorff took her picture in their apartment. She stands in front of a mirror, looking into it as she leans back on a desk. Her hair is long, pinned into a French roll.

I am shy about getting the details of how my parents fell in love. There are questions I don't ask. When did they first kiss? Where? What was it that attracted them to each other? I look at my mother and wonder all these things.

"She has very high expectations of men," Melly had written about her daughter in February of 1940. "Lore says, 'There won't be one like my daddy again and another one I don't want.' It will be difficult. Also he must understand something about ships. And he must earn money — not too little."

Many years before, in Vienna, Walter Wiener had written,

I dream of a woman with bright limbs
And blonde hair and a soft gentle hand,
A woman who can love.
With exultant songs I serenade her,
I embrace her and kiss her red lips.

Lore did not have blonde hair, and Walter understood little of ships. But in the summer of 1941, they frequently had dinner together with Lore's father in the Frensdorffs' apartment. After supper, when Walter got up to leave, Lore would often offer to accompany him part of the way home. Some-

times, without having intended to go so far, she found herself
in front of the house where he lived. Then he, in turn, insisted on seeing her back. But once there, Lore did not climb the
flight of stairs to her place. "Come," she said to Walter, "I'll
go with you to the corner…"

They spent these hot humid evenings of their first
months together walking along tree-lined boulevards with
French names. Route Prosper Paris, Avenue Joffre, Route
Alfred Magy, Tifeng Road and then again: Tifeng Road,
Route Alfred Magy, Avenue Joffre, Route Prosper Paris.

I have a map of Shanghai that the Asia Realty Company
issued in 1934. It is so large that when I spread it out, the blue
paper covers half of my desk. I trace along the streets with my
finger. I try to imagine what my parents experienced. The
rumble of rickshaw wheels on the street. The slap of the
coolies' bamboo sandals as they ran. The smell of peanut oil.
The breeze off the nearby Whangpoo River. I am just guessing.

One night in July, Lore had news for her father. "Daddy,"
she announced, "Walter and I are going to be married."

"But you can't!" her father exclaimed. "He's Jewish."

"And what about you?"

Willy Frensdorff said nothing. He smiled.

"He never mentioned it again," my mother tells me now.

It is years later. I am in an elevator with my parents in
New York. Something goes wrong. I sense the elevator will
fail. I get out and walk down the stairs. I do not alert my parents or urge them to leave the car. There is a public
announcement. Everything is under control. There is no reason to be afraid. I mistrust the announcement. And it turns
out that I am right to do so: the elevator plummets to the
ground. I rush over to see how my parents fared. My father is
walking slowly with a cane. He turns to me. I look searching-
ly into his mild blue eyes. He says, "I'm okay."

My mother is lying on the ground. She moves her head gingerly as if badly hurt. She starts to get to her feet. I tell her she should stay where she is, that perhaps she will make her injuries worse. She shakes her head, manages to stand, clinging to my father's arm.

"My father," she says, "also had great pain at the end."

But this accident does not happen. I dream it one August night in my bed under a blue-and-white paisley bedspread, my husband lying beside me asleep. The window is open. The blue-and-white curtains move slightly in the darkness and there's a faint smell of honeysuckle in the air. On one wall are black-and-white photographs of my husband's parents. On the wall behind my head is a large print of a picture called *The Kiss*. A kneeling black-haired man bends over a kneeling brown-haired woman. They wear golden robes. Her eyes are closed.

A few days afterwards I say to my husband, "It can't be a coincidence, having this elevator dream while I am writing about how my parents first saw each other in an elevator. Why do I get out? Why don't I try to help my parents? Why is my mother injured and my father unscathed? What does it mean?"

"What do you think?" asks Gordon.

"I don't know," I say, and remember something Talia said a few months before. "Everything in the world has gravity, even dreams," she informed me one afternoon while I was taking her to preschool. "Dreams have lots and lots of gravity. Things get split in two and then the gravity gets in." "How do you split a dream?" I asked. She said, "With a very sharp knife."

But whose knife is so sharp, I wonder now.

*Line drawing
of Willy
Frensdorff by
Kurt Marholz,
1947*

Something Missing

"Why do you think my grandfather didn't write anything about it?" I ask. "In Germany he used his diary even when things looked fairly hopeless."

I am sitting with my husband in our dining room at a five-sided cedar table not yet cleared of dessert dishes and teacups. Green streamers hang from the ceiling, left over from my daughter's fifth birthday party. A green papier-mâché octopus from the same party sits in the corner of the room. My daughter, Talia, is crouching inside a cardboard box on the floor near my chair. She pulls another cardboard box over her head.

"Mommy, look at me!" she shouts. "I'm hiding. Even my shadow has disappeared."

"No, it hasn't!" asserts my almost-seven-year-old son,

who is building a castle out of Kraft Dinner boxes and Campbell soup cans in the kitchen. "It's behind you."

Ignoring the children, I begin again. "Why do — "

"Mommy, I'm hiding," Talia interrupts. She takes the cardboard box off her head to make sure that I'm watching. I give up trying to talk.

My grandfather's last entries for the year 1941 marked anniversaries in November.

Nov. 10. Employment contract from S.P.C. [Shanghai Power Company] *1939.*

Nov. 14. First day at S.P.C. 1939.

In December, the spaces beside the printed dates are all blank. And after December 31, where a few pages were left free for notes, I don't see what I'm looking for either. I find a list of books Willy Frensdorff had borrowed from the library and another of books he had lent out. I learn that he had given my father *The Cheops Pyramids* and *Gespräche mit Einstein* (Discussions with Einstein). I see a series of quotations from Plato, Machiavelli, Pericles. I find the numbers that opened the combination lock on his safe; some liquor prices. But that's all.

So I don't know whether my grandfather heard the explosions on December 8, 1941, at 4:00 A.M. Was he woken by the sound of Japanese ships in the Whangpoo River firing upon a small British gunboat, the *Peterel*? And if he was, did he realize the significance of the noise? Or did he think, as some foreign residents did, that he was hearing a Chinese celebration with fireworks? Later, did he pick up one of the thousands of leaflets that planes had dropped on the city at dawn, urging everyone to stay calm? Did he go to the Shanghai Power Company on the morning of the eighth? At 10:00 A.M., did he see the Japanese troops streaming across the bridges spanning Soochow Creek? Did he watch as they marched onto the Bund, the embankment along the Whang-poo where so many Western businesses had their offices? Did he observe any of the sentries taking up positions in front of important foreign institutions — the British, American and Dutch consulates, the municipal building, the banks, cable offices and public utilities? Did he know that by noon the Settlement was completely in Japanese hands — that war had begun in the Far East?

"Do you remember what you were doing the day the Japanese came?" I ask my father while drinking tea and eating cookies in his kitchen.

At the time, my father was working for an English-language paper, the *North China Daily News*. He had left the *China Press* and taken the position of financial editor with the *Daily News* in August 1941. On December 7, a column of his appeared under the headline, "Shanghai public cheered by continued price control." He clipped the story and I have it now. Though yellow and stained, it is still legible. It begins, "While high politics continued rivetting the attention of Far Eastern observers during the past week, local residents had to go about the humble business of carrying on their day-to-day struggles for existence, Pacific crisis or no Pacific crisis....The first day of the week brought the glad tidings that the price of Hongay coal had been fixed by the authorities of the F.M.C. at $600 per ton, as compared with a price of $900 which had been quoted not so long ago."

"Did you go to work?" I ask. I know that the Japanese closed most of the English-language papers. "Did you see the soldiers arriving at the *North China Daily News*? And sealing the locks on the doors? Or did someone phone you and tell you not to come?"

"I can't quite recall," he says slowly.

My mother, who is listening, adds, "But you remember

some things so clearly! Last night you told me the name of your Russian landlady on Edinborough Road."

"I know — Yafdinsky. It's as if my brain is full of filing cabinets. And some of them I can't open."

"Were you afraid?" I ask them both.

"I don't remember fear," my mother answers. "Maybe it was because the soldiers didn't come into the French Concession where we lived."

The French authorities in Shanghai were pro-Vichy and therefore officially neutral. Out of respect for this status, the Japanese army did not actually enter the three square miles that France administered. This did not prevent their secret police from carrying out searches and arrests there, nor did it stop them from insisting that all foreigners register with the police. But it meant that Japanese power was a little less visible here than across Avenue Edouard VII in the Settlement.

My grandfather continued to work for the Shanghai Power Company, which the Japanese allowed to carry on under their supervision. (The Japanese did not shut other public utilities either — the Shanghai Telephone Company, the Waterworks and the Tramway Company kept running during the occupation.) My mother still designed clothes for Mrs. Stein, who ran My Lady's Salon on Avenue Pétain. My father, whose job with the newspaper disappeared, began to tutor private students, mostly in German. Willy and Lore kept their apartment on Route Prosper Paris, and because they both had incomes, they were able to retain the services of the Chinese cook they had hired earlier that year.

On December 24, 1941, sixteen days after Japanese flags began flying over the International Settlement, my parents were married. They had set the date months before. "I will make you a Christmas present for life," my mother had said to my father. They saw no reason to change their plans.

And so, on that Wednesday afternoon, six rickshaws moved swiftly down Route Prosper Paris. Twenty minutes later they stopped. Three men and three women alighted and went upstairs to a dark room carpeted with a Persian rug. They were in the home of the acting pastor of the Community Church of Shanghai. A woman dressed in a grey suit with fur cuffs and a man in navy blue exchanged marriage vows. Lore Frensdorff and Walter Wiener gave each other identical stainless steel rings engraved with a Greek key pattern. Willy Frensdorff, Annamarie and Carl Burchard, and Margaret Töpfer all signed the marriage certificate and then walked down the stairs to the waiting rickshaws. Along the darkening streets, they went back to Route Prosper Paris for a filet mignon dinner that the Frensdorffs' Chinese cook had prepared.

In Germany, Melly Frensdorff knew nothing of all this. She had moved back to Bremen from Goslar and was living in a boarding house run by a couple named Müller. On Richtweg in the centre of the city, her small room with a southern exposure overlooked the old city moat. From her balcony, she could see the Italian consulate with its large flag and Mussolini's slogan, "To believe, to obey and to fight."

After the Japanese occupied the International Settlement, Melly received no letters for about a year. The war in the Pacific had greatly disrupted the postal services. Finally, just before Christmas 1942, a Red Cross letter from Willy arrived. It was a short note, written on a special form that allowed no more than twenty-five words. "Guess you are now in the Harz; you would be a good help in Lore's business. Very happy with salary. Hope you are well. Trust in the little star," he wrote, closing with the words, "We three healthy."

Melly dispatched an equally short reply in February 1943. About her stepbrother she wrote, "Kurt Stalingrad no news." And about Willy's sister, "Clara a long time on the other side." I know from my mother that Clara had committed suicide by this time – with gas, in her apartment. But Melly left that part of the story out. She finished by asking about the other person that Willy had mentioned. "Your third?"

In July, Willy sent his wife another note saying they were all well, but he didn't answer her question. So in November she asked for a second time, "Who is your third?" Melly wrote to her husband again on New Year's Day, 1944. This time, she indicated that a letter had arrived by ordinary mail. It must have clarified something, for the same day Melly penned a note to my parents. But the letter she received clearly didn't elucidate everything: Melly still didn't know my father's name. She addressed him as "Dr. Walter" and my mother as "Lore Walter."

"I don't remember not telling her about getting married," my mother explains when we come to this series of letters. "I only remember not wanting to use the name 'Wiener.' Once, you know, I suggested to Daddy that we change the name. But he didn't want to. He said, 'Why should I? My parents were honourable people.'"

Later, I find some letters my grandmother wrote in 1948. The war had been over for three years. "It was unbelievable," one letter to my mother begins, "but yesterday I also received 3 packages from you, from November 1941....In them, I was informed that you two wanted to marry at Christmas because nothing else would do when you loved each other so madly. Your letter, despite its respectable age, had all the freshness of your twenty years. You wanted to carefully cultivate the flower of love – not too much and not too little water.

"These letters were postmarked Shanghai, February 1948. They sat patiently in some mailbag for seven years.

They were addressed to Müllers, Richtweg 4. The house doesn't exist any more. The Müllers moved to Harmel and then back here to two different addresses. They looked for me everywhere and finally found Frau Müller, who brought them to me."

"You see, we did try to tell her," my mother says.

One evening over dinner I tell Gordon about the letters that were delivered so late. I explain that it took almost two years for my grandmother to learn about my parents' wedding. And I say that I expected there to be a story behind this, maybe a secret. Perhaps that my parents had anticipated Melly's disapproval and so had not told her about their match. Lost letters seemed anticlimactic.

A couple of days after this conversation, Thomas brings home some French words and sentences he is supposed to learn for a dictation exercise. One of the sentences is, "*Au mois de novembre, il y a un secret.*" (In the month of November, there is a secret.)

"Where did that sentence come from?" I ask Thomas.

"I made it up," he informs me and grins. "Mme. Vézina used my sentence."

"What is the secret?"

"I don't know." Then he chuckles. "The secret is that there is no secret."

As it turns out, however, I do have something more to learn about my parents' life during the war. After December 1941, my grandfather made intermittent entries for four years, but they concerned war news only. He recorded the dates of battles, troop movements, conferences between wartime leaders. But he didn't mention himself or his family. Before, he had always recorded the birthdays of those close to him: Melly and Lore, his colleagues at the Ag. Weser and the Shanghai Power Company. Leafing through the diaries, it was easy to spot these entries. They were all under-lined with a red pencil. After December 1941, he didn't even note doctors' appointments or visits to the dentist. I wonder if he was worried that he or someone else might get into trou-ble if the diary fell into the wrong hands. And whose hands were the wrong ones? The Japanese *kempeitai* (the secret police in China)? Or did he fear their German counterparts, the Gestapo? And how could mentioning a birthday have led to difficulties anyway? Maybe he was too busy to write. Or too tired. It was almost as if he had effaced himself from the pages of his own diary. He didn't emerge again until two weeks after the war in Europe ended.

May 22, 1945. First postcard to Melly after hostilities stop.

The family photo albums show the same kind of gap. There are pictures labelled, "Prosper Paris, 1941." My moth-er sits beside a young dark-haired woman, a shelf of books above their heads. The Chinese cook, wearing a long white apron, stirs something in an enamel pot on a gas stove. Tommy, their black-and-white cat, looks away from the cam-era. And then "Tunsin Road, 1946." My father is sitting in a chair reading. My grandfather, wearing spats, scratches a black dog behind the ears. My mother stands in a courtyard with her hands on her hips, smiling in the sunshine.

What had happened during the intervening years?

Walter Wiener's Hongkew pass, 1946

Restricted Areas

After my parents' wedding, Walter moved into the Frensdorffs' apartment, and at the beginning of 1942 Lore painted the ceiling above their bed, first blue with silver stars and then white.

"What else do you remember of 1942?" I ask my mother.

"We had shoes made by a Chinese shoemaker in the Avenue Joffre," she says.

One day while we are talking it occurs to my parents that a friend of theirs, Roy Essoyan, might have more recollections about the Japanese occupation. He had moved to Shanghai with his Armenian parents as a boy and gone to school there. After graduating, he became a journalist, and in 1949 he took a job as correspondent with Associated Press. His Christmas cards to my parents over the years have always showed exotic return addresses – Cairo, Beirut, Hong Kong, Moscow. Now he is retired and lives in the uplands of Hawaii.

Six weeks after writing to him, I receive a reply. "The Japanese occupation of [the International Settlement in] Shanghai," Roy's letter goes, "was pretty sophisticated compared to Hong Kong, where the defense forces battled house to house for nearly three weeks, with thousands of casualties, before surrendering. In Shanghai, there was no defense, and the Japanese followed a kid glove policy, introducing each new restriction on our liberties in very small measures, and gradually, so as not to provoke a violent reaction.

"Enemy nationals were not even interned for more than a year until well into 1943, as I recall. They wore armbands, to identify them, and eventually our shortwave radios were ordered sealed, but freedom of movement was hardly restricted."

"It wasn't traumatic," my mother comments when I read Roy's letter to my parents.

I had always known that the Japanese had not interned my parents during the war. I thought this was because they were German and Austrian, that the Japanese had regarded them as *allies*. But now I know that the German Reich had stripped them of their citizenship and that they were stateless. Their documents read, "Expatriate German" and "Former Austrian citizen."

It is true that the Japanese did not treat my mother and father as "enemy nationals." My parents did not have to wear the red armbands that were issued to the British, Americans, Canadians and others in December of 1941. But neither did the Japanese consider them to be friends, like the Germans and Italians, or even neutrals, like the Portuguese and Greeks. They fell into yet another category – refugees.

I find a few books in the library that deal with the history of Jewish refugees in Shanghai: *The Fugu Plan* by Marvin

Tokayer and Mary Swartz, *Japanese, Nazis and Jews* by David Kranzler and *Wanderers and Settlers in the Far East* by Herman Dicker. Although the authors differ about details, essentially they tell the same story.

By 1942, the Germans were becoming increasingly irritated with the Japanese treatment of Asia's Jews. The final solution was in full swing everywhere in the German Reich, but in Shanghai 20,000 Jews were still free. So three high-ranking Nazis — Adolph Puttkammer, Hans Neumann and Colonel Meisinger — arrived to pressure Japanese authorities into following the German lead.

The Nazis had proposals. One was to build a concentration camp for Jews on Tsungming Island in the mouth of the Yangtze River. Another was to send them upriver to work in some salt mines. And a third was to set the Jews adrift at sea until they died. When the local Japanese vice-consul, Mitsugi Shibata, heard about these ideas, he did not like them at all. He passed the frightening news on to seven of Shanghai's most prominent Jews at a meeting in Michael Speelman's living room.

The men were incredulous. But they were relieved to learn that Tokyo was not behind the proposals. It was possible, they reasoned, that the Nazi plans could be stopped if more senior Japanese officials were told about them.

The Jewish men decided to send a message to Dr. Abraham Kaufman, who lived in Harbin, a city to the northeast. Kaufman was on friendly terms with a couple of influential Japanese, namely Yosuke Matsuoka, the former foreign minister, and Norihiro Yasue, an advisor to the government in Manchuko. The seven community leaders also agreed to enlist the help of Fritz Brahn. Brahn, who also was Jewish, had an aristocratic Japanese girlfriend who knew the chief of the kempeitai.

Weeks passed and nothing happened. Then Brahn had his meeting with the chief of the kempetai. Unfortunately, Brahn revealed who had been at the meeting in Speelman's house, and within forty-eight hours all the men who had been there, including Shibata, found themselves in Bridge House, a notorious prison. They were beaten, and one man was severely tortured. But eventually all eight were let go. Shibata was sent back to Japan. When the Jews were released, the prison sergeant lectured them. The Japanese, he said, were their protectors and would do them no harm. How could they have thought otherwise?

None of the Nazis' plans ever fully materialized. However, the Japanese were willing to accommodate the German wishes at least this far: they would segregate the majority of the Jews from the rest of the population. "In November 1942," Tokayer relates, "a top secret dispatch was sent from the Japanese consul general in Shanghai, Seiki Yano, to Kazuo Aoki, minister of Greater East Asia: 'A Jewish district will be set up in the Hongkew area. The Jewish people scattered within the city will be collected together in order to live in this district. Surveillance, control and guidance will be a military function.'"

In January 1943, the Japanese government began interning the enemy nationals, about 10,000 people, in seven enclosures around Shanghai. In February, they turned to the refugees. On the eighteenth, the commander of the Imperial Japanese Navy and the commander of the Imperial Army jointly issued a proclamation that was published on posters, broadcast over radio stations and printed in all of Shanghai's newspapers. Stateless refugees were required to move their residences and their businesses to a part of the International Settlement known as Hongkew. The area was limited on the west by Chaofoong, Muirhead and Dent roads, on the east by the Yangtzepoo Creek, on the south by East Seward and Way-side roads, and on the north by the boundary to the Settle-ment. The refugees had three months to move. If they did not, they would be punished.

"The Japanese," Tokayer and Swartz relate, "did not carry out a pogrom — instead, they created the first Jewish ghetto in Asia." Strangely enough, however, they did not use the word "ghetto." They referred to a "designated area" and a "restricted area." The proclamation did not mention Jews, either. The Japanese considered a "stateless refugee" to be a person who had no citizenship and had arrived in Shanghai after 1937 from Germany (including the former Austria and Czechoslovakia), Hungary, the former Poland, Latvia, Lithuania or Estonia. This naturally excluded those Germans who had arrived since 1937 but who were not Jewish and still retained their citizenship. It also excluded all the White Rus-sians and the 4000 Russian Jews who lived in Shanghai. Although many of them had no citizenship papers either, the proclamation did not mention them. Tokayer and Swartz point out that the Japanese had signed a mutual neutrality pact with Stalin in the middle of 1941 and were reluctant to do anything that might imperil the accord.

After finishing *The Fugu Plan*, I phone my mother to describe it to her. We discuss the Nazis' proposals a little first. I ask if she had heard about them. She has a dim recollection of them, she says, although the names Puttkammer, Neu-mann and Meisinger are unfamiliar. Then I inquire, "Did you have to go to Hongkew?" She affirms that she, my father and my grandfather did. "It might have been possible for my daddy to stay out because of his job with the Power Compa-ny. But he didn't want to live by himself."

Although what my mother says is new to me, I don't write anything in my diary about our conversation. Later this will both annoy and surprise me. I don't have the same reasons to be afraid that my parents and grandfather had. Yet, as I investigate the events that my family did not talk about for so long, it is apparently difficult for me to keep track of my reactions. Sometimes I think it is hard for me to remain fully conscious of what I am doing. I don't have to worry about the secret police. But my diary, like my grandfather's, has gaps.

A couple of weeks after talking to my mother about *The Fugu Plan*, I learn more about Hongkew from my father. He explains the pass system to me. The Japanese allowed refugees to leave Hongkew during working hours if they had a job elsewhere in the city. But to do so passes were required. The man who issued them, K. Ghoya, was a petty tyrant who used his power to terrorize people. "In the designated area," my father says, "you were half a prisoner, half free."

Then my mother starts to read *The Fugu Plan* herself. One day she phones to tell me I shouldn't get the idea that their life in Shanghai had been as miserable or frightening as some of the lives depicted in the book. She, my father and my grandfather all worked outside the ghetto. This meant that they had some freedom of movement as well as a steady income. Then she tells me something I find unsettling. She says that my father was a policeman during the time they were living in Hongkew, a *Pao Chia* man. I wonder what he had to do. Something that he later regretted? There were Jewish policemen in the ghettos in Europe too. They were often regarded as turn-coats or traitors. Was my father?

All male refugees between twenty and forty, my mother recounts, were required to take turns guarding the entrances to the ghetto. They had to make sure that those leaving had permission to do so. If anyone returned after the curfew fell, the Pao Chia man was supposed to report the incident to the Japanese authorities. "Did Daddy ever have to do that?" I ask.

"I don't think so," my mother says.

I feel relieved. I am certain he would have hated to do it. About a week later, I am visiting my parents' house. I say to my father, "Mommy tells me you were a Pao Chia man." His eyes widen and he nods. "Did you ever have to turn anyone over to the Japanese?"

"No, there was never anything like that."

My uneasiness subsides a little.

In my parents' black trunk is a piece of paper called the "Pao Chia Census Form." According to it, Willy Frensdorff, Walter Wiener and Lore Wiener left their three-room apartment in the French Concession for a place at 305/31 Kunping Road on May 17, one day before the deadline expired. My grandmother didn't know about the move until after the war. In his Red Cross notes to her, Willy gave the Shanghai Power Company as his return address. He never mentioned Kunping Road.

Willy, Lore and Walter brought with them two beds, a table, a chair and their big black-and-white cat, Tommy. My mother remembers that the tiny space they took on the third floor of a house was about three metres square. To provide a place for them, a Polish refugee, Harens Pels, divided a room he had rented for himself and his daughter, Stella. There was a partition made of plywood stained a mahogany brown, with a blue painted frame. The room did not have its own entrance. To get to it, one walked into Mr. Pels's side of the partitioned room and through a sliding wooden door. On the other side, a single window overlooked a red tiled roof, and Tommy used it as a cat door. A yellow curtain was pulled at night to create separate sleeping spaces. The bathroom was on the floor below, and the kitchen, which my family shared with Mr. Pels, was tucked under some stairs. There was no space for the piano my grandfather had rented a year earlier.

Although the room was barely big enough for Willy, Lore and Walter, they were happy to get it. Even before the proclamation was issued, Hongkew was crowded. It was already home to 100,000 Chinese and 8000 refugees who were attracted by the low rents and cheap prices in the district. The proclamation meant that another 8000 people had to obtain accommodation there somehow. Finding anything at all was a scramble.

In 1943, Shanghai was a city on the move. My mother drew comfort from the fact that her family wasn't the only one affected. "I wasn't too worried," she tells me, "because everyone was going somewhere. Our English and American friends were moving to internment camps. I remember a cocktail party in the Picardie Apartments just before we left for Hongkew. The Braidwoods were there and they were about to leave for camp too. I think if we had been singled out, it would have been more disturbing."

Certainly there were protests. The Polish Jews, in particular, tried vigorously to make a case against the relocation order. They argued that the Japanese proclamation had never mentioned Jews but had everywhere used the euphemism "stateless refugees." The Poles maintained that they were not stateless, since there was a Polish government-in-exile in London that recognized their citizenship. The authorities were unmoved. Eventually, according to David Kranzler's book *Japanese, Nazis and Jews*, all but about fifty of the refugees took up residence in Hongkew.

My parents tell me that one of these fifty was my uncle, Günther Wiener, who never lived in the "designated area." But when I ask them how he managed to stay out, they are unable to remember. I write to my uncle asking the same question, and his reply is prompt as usual.

"Since the arrival of your writing I'm turning our house

upside down to find diverse papers to explain to you why I didn't have to move to Hongkew in 1943. I suppose this question interests you more than anything else. In 1943, I applied for Soviet citizenship at the Soviet Embassy in Shanghai. I received a paper called *spravka*. With this document I got an exception from the Japanese. I really was lucky."

It was the Japanese delicacy of language that helped my uncle. If the proclamation had referred to Jews, he would not have been able to avoid its terms. But since it applied to stateless refugees only, his strategem of acquiring Soviet citizenship worked.

The next time I see my father, I say, "Do you know why your brother didn't have to move to Hongkew?" I am very excited. I don't wait for his reply but immediately start reading my uncle's letter out loud.

"I had no idea," my father tells me, when I stop reading.

"Today I saw in the weather forecast," my uncle's letter ends, "Vancouver had in the morning rain and 10 degrees Celsius. The world became very small."

The Garden Bridge leading out of Hongkew

14

In the Bamboo Box

Years before, my father had told me about Eva Lee. She was a girl he had tutored in Shanghai. Her mother was German and her father, a wealthy chemist, was Chinese. She wrote stories, my father said. One day, among his papers, I come across a notebook of hers, dated October 1944 to May 1945.

Eva wrote the stories in German, but she scribbled the words to English songs on the covers of the booklet. "Night and you and blue Hawaii. The night is heavenly and you are heaven to me." She repeated the title of a Glenn Miller classic, *In the Mood*, several times. And in the margins, beside the German stories, she added Chinese characters.

Many of the stories summarize what Eva had learned from history books she had been reading. "After a long journey, we finally reached the Danube" — so begins an account of some adventures experienced by a chaplain who served a German king centuries earlier. But there are also some stories she invented. One of them has a strange fascination for me.

"Splendid were the days when we went to visit my uncle in Peking. He lived in a house with many rooms and halls in which my cousins and I used to dance until late into the evening. One day there was a party to which everyone was invited. We played banjos, ukuleles, guitars, castanets. We really had a perfect Hawaiian band. As the party drew to a close, I was allowed to choose a song for the finale. Naturally, I chose *In the Mood*, my favourite. The Hawaiian band played it very well. We danced the much-loved fox trot. Suddenly, in the middle of the dance, I felt something hollow under my feet. I let a handkerchief drop and made a cross with my nail on the spot.

"As our little coconut party, as we called it, came to an end, we said 'Aloha' and 'Hasta la vista' to each other. I took my guitars, my ukuleles, my banjo and my castanets to my room. Then I returned to the ballroom where the Hawaiian band was packing up and about to leave. When they were gone, I went quickly to the certain spot and tried to lift up the boards. After many vain attempts, I finally succeeded. I found a large bamboo box that opened easily. In it was a scroll. With curiosity, I unrolled it and saw a magnificent painting in front of me. It showed a king's palace, most wonderfully appointed. The colours were so beautifully painted that I couldn't stop looking at it. After a lengthy investigation, I discovered a signature. Finally, I recognized the name 'Ku k'ai chih.' I remembered that two years ago, our tutor, Dr. Wiener, taught us that this was a renowned Chinese painter. Overjoyed, I ran to Papa and showed it to him."

I keep thinking about Eva in that fictional ballroom in Peking. Is it because I too have a box in which something is hidden? And because, like Eva, I cannot stop looking at the contents? Or is it the strange coincidence that, in the story, my father helps her to understand what she has found?

I become curious about the meaning of the Chinese characters in the notebook. I show them to an acquaintance of mine, Violet Redl, who can read them.

"The calligraphy is good, but it doesn't make sense," she says. "Green, silk, lake, palm," she reads. And then, "Don't go in by the back door."

"Perhaps she was just practising," Violet suggests.

I want to know about Ku k'ai chih. Was he real? I look up the name in my encyclopedia and am startled to find a reference. It is almost like learning that a mythical beast can be seen in the local zoo. My *Britannica* informs me that Ku k'ai chih lived between 344 and 406 A.D. He was the most important post-Han dynasty painter and worked at the Chin court in Nanking. There is even a reproduction of one of his scrolls, unfortunately not in colour. "A court lady glides forward to protect an emperor from an onrushing bear and is herself rescued by the guards," says the description.

Now when I imagine Hongkew I picture Eva too, a richly coloured counterpoint. Somehow she makes it easier to think about those crowded buildings and dreary treeless streets. Eva is an escape for me. She was for my father, too. In her Chinese house with its heavy carved furniture, her father, Dr. Lee, walked along the polished floors in a long gown and navy-blue silk shoes. Eva and her sister giggled about their aunts' jowly faces, and servants brought tea. My father could talk about Chinese painting and elucidate German grammar. For a while, he could forget the designated area with its fence made of barbed wire and rope.

The exits to Hongkew were always guarded, either by Japanese sentries or by men like my father who were required to assist them. In case anyone did not understand what the sentries and the barbed wire meant, there were signs. White letters, all capitals, on a dark background. They said, in English, "STATELESS REFUGEES ARE PROHIBITED TO PASS HERE WITHOUT PERMISSION."

Willy, Lore and Walter were lucky. They were able to obtain special passes to leave the ghetto. According to Anna Ginsbourg, writing in the November 17, 1945, edition of the *China Weekly Review*, these passes were valid for a period of one to six months. "The shorter time-limit [was] usually imposed so as to give the refugees the maximum amount of inconvenience."

Willy Frensdorff got someone called H. Oura in the staff office of the Japanese Military Controlled Shanghai Power Company to sign letters applying for his pass. Written in English and identically worded, they are typed on Power Company letterhead and addressed to the Shanghai Stateless Refugees Affairs Bureau. In the middle of each letter, the words "Application for prolongation of the Special Pass" are underlined. Some details are given. The pass is blue and its number is 20. William Frensdorff is described as an Assistant Engineer with a monthly salary of C.R.B. $7,408.09.

Most of the letters are dated, but three are copies with a blank space after "Date:". My grandfather probably made carbons to save typing a new letter every three months. They are ready to be used again, I think. It is an unpleasant idea.

For Walter Wiener, there is just one such letter. Dated March 31, 1943, it addresses S.A.C.R.A., the Shanghai Ashkenazi Collaborating Relief Association: "I hereby apply for a special pass to leave the designated area for the purpose of attending to my daily duties." My father then explains that he is employed by Mr. Z. V. Coblenz and Mrs. L. Montanaro in the capacity of a private teacher. He closes the letter with his unfailing politeness. "I beg to remain, Sirs, Yours sincerely, Walter Wiener."

I find no such letter for Lore Wiener. But her pass still exists, a small card about three inches by five. She smiles in the photograph – the picture was taken in Vienna in 1939. Fourteen dates are stamped on the pass. The first is March 1944, the last, August 1945. The red ink has smudged, making the card pink.

K. Ghoya, a small and exceedingly ugly man, distributed the passes. "It always took more than half a day to get them," recalls my mother. "Some people brought folding chairs or stools with them." The applicants waited in long lines in the corridor outside Ghoya's office, staring at the reddish-pink walls and wondering about the Japanese official's mood. When he was angry, he slapped people.

Anna Ginsbourg writes, "Statistics show about 30,000 pass renewals for 3000 refugees during the whole period, and with two out of every three applicants receiving slaps as well as renewals, the official slap-administering record of the bureau stands at at least 20,000."

My father tells me a story about one occasion on which he was waiting to have his pass renewed. "A friend of mine, Alfred Jacobi, was in the line too. That day Ghoya was in a particularly bad mood, hitting people left and right. Dr. Jacobi said loudly, 'He can't touch me. I was an officer in the German army.' My friend was Prussian, you see, and quite proud. Unfortunately Ghoya overheard the remark, and though he didn't say anything, I could see that he flinched. When it was Dr. Jacobi's turn, of course Ghoya slapped him."

"Were you ever slapped?" I inquire.

My parents shake their heads. "I was lecturing at St. John's University," my father explains. "Ghoya saw this and asked me whether I knew a Professor Sekya who was teaching comparative religion there. I told him that I did. He smiled, said, 'Fine man,' and stamped my pass. I never had any trouble after that."

"It wasn't too bad," adds my mother. "At least Ghoya didn't kill anyone."

"What was the worst thing that happened while you were living in Hongkew?" I ask.

"There was the time my daddy's wallet was stolen, with his monthly salary in it. Afterwards, he sat at our table with his head in his hands, saying 'What do we do now?' Your daddy went to the shop where we bought our groceries and arranged for one month's credit.

"And once I was somewhere outside Hongkew with my daddy. It was late, time for us to be back. My daddy began to complain of chest pains. He wanted to rest. 'We've got to get going,' I kept saying. 'I can't!' he said. I more or less dragged him along. Later I realized he had probably suffered a mild heart attack. At the time, my only thought was to get in before the curfew."

Talking to my parents, I have the impression that they lived in a kind of safety zone. Although there were difficulties, in many ways life went on much as before. Every morning during the week, Willy caught the streetcar to go to his office, still at its old location on 181 Nanking Road. Lore went to My Lady's Salon on Avenue Pétain in the French Concession. The owner of the store, Mrs. Stein, gave my mother orders for garments. Then Lore paid a group of Chinese tailors to sew her designs. She still remembers some of the clothes. "They had short skirts, tight waists and broad padded shoulders — a military look. Once I made a dress for myself out of Chinese cotton with a white scrolly pattern down the front. Everyone wanted to have one."

Walter rode a bicycle to the houses of his students and to

the St. John's University campus on the outskirts of the International Settlement. In the spring of 1943, he taught a course called Economics 108. His students were mostly Chinese, but the language of instruction was English. The spring term final exam had questions such as, "What is the social function of saving?" and "What are the factors determining the distribution of the money flow, and which of these factors is important for the development of a so-called vertical maladjustment?"

It sounds so normal. But when I talk to other people I get a sense of how narrow was the zone of safety in which my family lived.

Ingrid Wilmot has an attractively throaty voice with a trace of a mid-European accent. We met through an Old China Hands Reunion held in Vancouver in July of 1992. Ingrid lives in California. A couple of months after the reunion, I phone her to talk about Hongkew. Like my father, she came to Shanghai from Vienna in 1938, although she was much younger than he, still a girl. In 1943, she and her family were also forced to move to Hongkew. She was by then a teen-ager.

"One day I had a special pass," Ingrid recalls, "to leave Hongkew to go to the funeral of my boyfriend's mother."

But on her return she became lost.

"I didn't realize that the Japanese had put barricades around the Bund area. They did it because of the Italian ship, the *Conte Verde*. The Italians had sunk it in the harbour. [The crew members scuttled the ship when their king surrendered to the Allies in 1943; they didn't want it to fall into the hands of the Japanese, who had become their enemies.] The Japanese had been trying for two years to get the ship up. They couldn't do it, and it was such an embarrassment that they fenced off the Bund. They didn't want people to see the ship.

I didn't know how to get past all the barbed wire and onto the Garden Bridge. I noticed a Chinese guy stepping over some pipes. I thought he looked like he knew where he was going and I followed him. Suddenly a Japanese sentry appeared."

The Chinese fellow turned and ran away, but Ingrid stayed where she was. She thought that the sentry might be able to help her find the way back to Hongkew.

"The sentry started yelling at me. They were always yelling. And then he cut my neck with his bayonet and sliced at the sleeves of my coat. I could feel the warm blood trickling down. Out of nowhere, a tall Sikh policeman turned up. I began explaining my problem to him. 'Let me, let me,' he said. He started talking to the sentry in Japanese and gestured for me to go.

"I was scared to death, but somehow I managed to get onto the Garden Bridge. I ran really fast. I ran all the way home. It was a long way, but I made it."

When she got back, her mother opened the door and fainted at the sight of her daughter drenched in blood. "I fainted too," says Ingrid.

Then she remembers another story, this one about her father, Hugo Fried. He was the part-owner of a restaurant called the Barcelona. Towards the end of the war, when things began to go against them, the Japanese administration became harsher and stricter. The authorities insisted that Mr. Fried was allowing political meetings to take place in the Barcelona.

"One night, there was a raid. The Japanese chased everyone out and declared the restaurant to be off limits," explains Ingrid. "For six months, no one came in. People were afraid they would get into trouble. But then customers began drifting back. The Japanese raided the place again. This time they took all the men, including my father, away in a truck to a prison of some kind. There they tied my father's hands and hung him up on a wall. As he hung there, his pant leg began to creep up, exposing a scar from an old World War I shrapnel wound. I remember that scar well. It was as smooth as glass. As a kid, I used to love to touch it. The Japanese officer in charge noticed this, bent down and pulled up his own pant leg. He had a fresh shrapnel wound in exactly the same place as my father's. He gave an order for my father to be taken down."

The next day, when Ingrid's mother arrived at the prison with food, her father was allowed to leave.

"It's strange," says Ingrid. "In some ways, I hate the Japanese more than the Germans. Although I cried for three days when we left Vienna, I bounced back. We survived, things turned out all right. We weren't starving, we had lots of friends. In the beginning, my father's business went well. But when the Japanese came, it was the nightmare all over again. This time, I was older and understood better what was going on. I was sure they'd get us in the end.

"I understand they almost did. But then they started to lose the war. They were too busy defending themselves to do anything about us. It was horrible."

My mother, though, says, "It wasn't so bad."

What does it all mean? I am in the car with Gordon, driving to a movie, a rare treat. The children are away for the weekend. I say, "I keep wondering how Hongkew influenced my parents' lives."

We stop at a red light. Gordon turns to look at me and says, "It just struck me that your uncle was the one who told you about your grandmother and he was the one who didn't go to Hongkew." Was it really Hongkew that made the difference? Is that why there was so much my parents didn't tell me?

Lore Wiener,
Hangchow,
April 1947

15

Finally Free

May 1945. American planes flew out of the north in a V-for-
mation. Walter, Lore and Willy were happy they were coming. Nevertheless, when they heard the air-raid sirens, they
sought shelter with their neighbours, the Kramers. Mrs.
Kramer was a music teacher and she had a grand piano.
Lacking any better protection, they all sat under it and sang.

On August 15, the high-pitched voice of the Japanese
emperor was broadcast over the loudspeakers hanging above
the streets throughout Shanghai. People on the streets stood
still to listen. The speech was hard to understand, even for
the Japanese, because it was highly formal. But somehow the
message came through. Japan had surrendered.

Within days, Walter heard about a vacant apartment on
the top floor of a house on the outskirts of Shanghai. When

he visited it, he saw that it had two large rooms as well as a kitchen and a bathroom. High-ceilinged and airy with generous dormer windows, the apartment was built to catch the breeze. It was palpably cooler here than downtown.

He told the landlord that he would like to take it immediately. Delighted with his discovery, he raced back to Kunping Road and arranged for a truck to come that afternoon. He lost no time looking for packing boxes. Instead, he knotted the family's possessions – clothing, household linens, books and papers – into a couple of sheets. Then Walter phoned Lore and Willy at work. He told them that he had rented a new place to live and was moving everything. They should go directly to 150 Tunsin Road. There was no need to return to their old room.

When the driver arrived, Walter helped to load the two beds, a chair and a table onto the back of the pickup. He balanced the sheets on top of the furniture and rode out of Hongkew holding the cat, Tommy, in his arms.

"Perhaps I should have had one last look around, but I never went back," says my mother. "I didn't keep in contact with Mr. Pels and his daughter either. I think I heard that she went to New York."

The apartment on Tunsin Road was a lucky find. Although the rent was high – $75 U.S. monthly – the landlord had not asked for any "key money," an exorbitant sum customarily demanded of new tenants. After the tiny room in Hongkew, it seemed spacious. The house was white, with a steep shingled roof and shuttered windows. A broad street curved in front of it and there were hedges and trees. Except for the bamboo fence, it might almost have been an English cottage.

The only person who was not enthusiastic about the move was Lore's head tailor. "Missy, you can't move in there," he said. "The house no good for *lao tou zi*!" He was talking about Willy Frensdorff; the Chinese term meant "old master." "*Lao tou zi* always die there," the tailor explained.

But my mother wasn't worried. The family settled in. The photographs begin again. Pictures of my mother on Tunsin Road show a smiling woman with thick, dark hair down to her shoulders. She wears slim knee-length skirts, blouses with mandarin sleeves and sensible shoes. My father has loose-fitting shirts, baggy pants and sometimes an ascot. His smile is not so broad as my mother's. My grandfather has a light tropical suit. A black dog, part lab, called Jackie, has joined the household. In several photographs, Willy pats Jackie or holds him with a leash.

My grandmother mailed a letter to my father at the new apartment. She forgot to date it, but I know that she wrote after the war because she sent it to 150 Tunsin Road. I also know that she had finally learned his name: she addressed the envelope to Dr. Walter Wiener.

"My dear son-in-law," Melly began. "What an unusual coincidence, but a nice and welcome one, that we are compatriots.... And if you stand between the nations, it is quite the same for me because which nation I belong to now is not clear. I was until my sixteenth year Viennese, then 8 years in Trieste, which even at that time was more Italian than Austrian, then 25 years in northern Germany, finally since 1933 sort of Jewish. Where should I take a precise national feeling from? I have a great inclination to be a world citizen."

In October 1945, Lore decided to open her own store. She rented a shop on the ground floor of the Picardie, an exclusive apartment building on the Avenue Pétain. "Lore Maria Wiener" was painted in gothic letters on the window. "Haute Couture and Individual Designs."

Walter began to write on a freelance basis for a newsmagazine, the *China Weekly Review*. A November 1945 editorial of his entitled "A New Deal for Shanghai" began, "In taking a factual inventory of the local situation two months after V-J day, we find prices have reached a new high, living conditions are harder and unemployment has increased, while corruption and inefficiency appear as deep-rooted as ever."

A picture shows him with John Powell, the son of the *Review*'s owner. They are seated at a polished wooden desk scattered with issues of the magazine. Behind them is a shelf of reference books and a map on the wall titled "100 Years of War." Two Chinese men stand beside them, one wearing a Western suit and tie and the other dressed in a long Chinese gown.

In January 1946, Walter got his old position back at the *North China Daily News*. R. T. Peyton-Griffin, who had spent the last two years of the war in Haiphong House, a Japanese prison, had returned as editor-in-chief.

Willy Frensdorff began to think about how he could be reunited with his wife. "Sept. 21, 1946. My dear Melly: I, for my part, after having read your tempting descriptions, would happily go home, but I am not old enough just to watch how the radishes and potatoes grow. You know how it is with me, I have to have an absorbing occupation, otherwise I am not satisfied."

He planned to bring Melly to Shanghai, where they would live together for a few years. They would sail back to Bremen once conditions in Germany had improved. Now there were many shortages, particularly of food, and Willy frequently sent packages of basic supplies to Melly.

"Oct. 5, 1946. My dear Melly: I would wish for not too large a ship, many ports to visit and about two months at sea in which to wend our way home slowly. Oh, Melly, when I imagine something like that, I can hardly believe it! But we want to enjoy it together in all comfort, not like my emigration, the test run. How wonderful it would be to finally be on board ship, to call into a calm harbour, to go for a constitutional every morning in the sunshine. I'm looking forward to it even now. I haven't forgotten my seamanship and I still like to watch navigation from the bridge.

"And when we arrive home, the roses will be blooming, the fruit trees will be magnificent and we can contemplate the past with satisfaction. Then I would be ready to watch the radishes grow — if it is not out of bitter need. Your Willy."

Willy never mentioned the civil war that was raging across China in his letters. The Communists were gaining control of the railways and capturing important cities in the north. But the threat must have seemed distant. He wanted to stay on a few more years. So did Walter and Lore.

"Oct. 13, 1946. Dear gracious lady," my father wrote to the mother-in-law he had never met, "Lore has already told me so much about you that it sometimes seems to me that we are old acquaintances. I can readily understand your attachment to Europe and Bremen. I often deeply regret that I had to leave the Viennese landscape and atmosphere. But what can one do? War and politics are, after all, powerful influences. At the moment we are making so many plans and are racking our brains over the perpetual dilemma: stay or go? We, that is, Lore and I, believe it would be good to save some money and then to leave Asia. Your W. H. Wiener."

After six years in China it was not easy to think about going. "We are, in a way, tied to this patch of earth by financial considerations, to be sure, but without those one doesn't get by nowadays," Willy wrote to Melly that fall. "Lore's business is in an excellent location because really only solid, rich people live there. You have to realize that, here in Shanghai, to have a store already means an asset of $10,000 U.S. Just today Lore bought fabric intended for the new store and the Christmas trade. The business was all built up without a cent of debt, only the original foundation of my salary at the Power Company. When I remember how 6 years ago we had to pay for her sewing machine in gold dollars, how we stretched ourselves to extract it from my salary!"

On New Year's Day, 1947, my grandfather saw the movie *Fantasia*. My father attended a party for the staff of the *North China Daily News*. A picture of the event shows people holding glasses or small cups. Although they are indoors, they are all wearing their winter coats; my father's has a fur collar. In front of them is a wooden table covered in a sheet of white paper. There are bottles of champagne and rice wine, and loaves of sliced white bread.

Early that spring, my grandfather decided to get a piano again. In his diary, he recorded that the rent was $7 U.S. a month. He noted that to transport the piano to his house had cost him 120,000 Nationalist dollars and to have the piano tuned was 50,000 dollars. The inflationary pressure on the local currency was already so great that a U.S. dollar traded for about 7000 Nationalist dollars.

Nevertheless, my parents seemed unconcerned. In April, they went for a week's vacation to Hangchow, a resort town to the south of Shanghai, about five hours away by train. Photographs show old stone walls, water, bridges, fruit trees in bloom. Buddhist monks stroll beside great stone urns. My mother looks pensively over the back of a carved wooden bench towards an expanse of water.

Willy had been trying to obtain a visitor's visa for Melly. When his efforts failed, a colleague of his at the Power Company offered to enlist the help of his wife's influential grandfather in Nanking. In June, Willy learned from this man that getting a permit was bound up with many complications. But Willy was optimistic. He wrote to Melly that the colleague's wife promised to speak to her grandfather again on her next visit to Nanking.

By the middle of summer, the heat and humidity had become oppressive — 32°C in Willy's office and 30° in the apartment. How miserable Melly would have been, Willy thought. He had believed that because of the food shortages in Germany she would be better off in China. But now that he was able to send her packages regularly, he was no longer worried by "the spectre of starvation." He wrote, "I can't justify plaguing you to come here again. As for me, I can't decide when to go back but it is a source of great satisfaction that I am completely free in this matter and my own man. Once I have decided to go back, then there is naturally no return.... Above all, what restrains me from returning home are the Nazi-educated boys. Some time must pass before these guys are cured. Why should I risk the possibility of being together with such riffraff again?...Now we have time and can wait."

The terrible heat wave continued. Willy was amazed that he had forgotten how uncomfortable the summers were. The thought of an early return began tempting him. He had not been sleeping well and wondered whether eight years in the tropics were too much for a man of his age. "I am fed up!" he wrote in English. He planned to make an appointment with a Dr. Goldschmidt during his October holidays to ask if the doctor would recommend a change of climate for health reasons.

Although he did not plan to leave imminently, he intended to gradually prepare for departure. "I won't hurry myself, but perhaps I won't have to sweat here next summer. What actually held me in Shanghai was that I wanted to do as much as I could to build a nest for Lore and Master. [He was referring to my father, whom the Chinese servants called Young Master.] The Moor has done his duty.

"Perhaps the Americans can use me there, because I am without a doubt a person who brings with him no Nazi inclinations.... To use nautical language, it is like a regatta when one has decided to tack and go home with the spinnaker and full sail. So, fair winds and fondest wishes. Your Willy."

The heat exceeded all the forecasts. According to the Chinese calendar, it was fall. But Willy was often drenched in sweat. He decided to sail back to Germany the following May. "In the morning one isn't refreshed and staggers back into the treadmill. That will come to an end next year, now that I have firmly decided to return.... I won't bring cash with me, because one is only allowed to take $100 (U.S.). Instead, I will get us well outfitted — so that we will have enough for our old age and I won't have worked in vain for 8 years. I will have my black coat with the velvet collar lined with fur and a good warm winter suit made. I will also bring fur-lined gloves for you and for me. I am afraid that I will be very sensitive to the winter cold because here one freezes when the temperature reaches 0.

"The last former Nazi party members who were able to keep from being repatriated will now be forced to go home. It would be funny if I went home on the same ship as these gentlemen. I have no desire to see them and would rather be alone. Your Willy."

The August heat was relentless, without any sign of a summer typhoon, which usually brought cooler weather. "In the morning I wake up with weary bones....I am always thinking about next year. It makes it a little more bearable.... Despite the sweltering heat I am in the best of moods. I attribute this to the fact that I feel myself freer than I have for a long time in my life. I am probably influenced by the thought that I will finally breathe the sea air again. A fish that experimented with 8 years on land will now breathe through its gills again.

"German doesn't have the word 'smart.' Well, the hoodlum, Hitler, didn't do what he wanted, which was to harm me. He wasn't 'smart' enough.... Your Willy."

At the end of August, another engineer at the Power Company commented on Willy's good mood. "Why are you so jolly?" he asked. "You are usually so awfully serious."

Willy said, "It's because I'm going home next year."

"Is that so?" remarked the colleague. "Next year is still a long way away."

But Willy's spirits were undampened. "What finally brought me to the decision," he explained in his next letter to Melly, "was the prospect of different air and less odour, thinking of the Westerland. There we have it — not the 'homeland,' not the 'fatherland,' clichés that don't call the child by its correct name. We Germans don't have the right word for it. The Englishman speaks of his 'country,' an expression that doesn't have such a political flavour — the land where I was born and where I was happy, not because of the people but because of the landscape. Lore would interject, 'Don't be so sentimental,' but everyone is, only some are embarrassed to admit it. Some people lie unconsciously, because they are afraid or ashamed to express their innermost feelings, to clothe them in words. That is how it begins. It becomes a habit, and then in the end one can't do anything else, one gets stuck in a mood that one can only escape with difficulty. That is stupid, sometimes certainly mental laziness. Enough. I am merry because I have finally made myself free, acknowledging my shyness. Your Willy."

I know that my grandfather was not a demonstrative man. My mother has spoken of this. He was from northern

Germany, she said, by way of explanation. It was typical of the people there. But now I see that some of that reserve may also have come from his political situation; he was so vulnerable. My mother had alluded to his lack of anger. I think that he did not allow himself to express it — perhaps he did not even allow himself to feel it. But when the danger was over, he could call Hitler a hoodlum and his followers riffraff. I think it is no accident that, at the same time, other feelings seemed to be awakening in him. He could drop the habit of concealing himself. The war was over; the Americans had liberated Shanghai. Now Willy Frensdorff could liberate himself.

"Sept. 7. My dear Melly: The balance is not bad, and with our houses, our thrift and the combined savings, I think in our old age we will be secure and independent. When I look back that is really quite an achievement. After all, the Nazis were not smart enough to destroy us. Your Willy."

Two days later, Willy noted a fever of 38.6°C in his diary. He was suffering from what seemed to be a flu. Two weeks later, his fever continued unabated. The fluctuations in his temperature are recorded in Willy's diary not in his neat, small script but in a larger, rounder one — his nurse's. On September 26, his temperature dropped to 36.3°C, but four days later he was dead. The doctor told my mother that tuberculosis baccilli had entered his bloodstream.

My mother remembers sobbing. She remembers being in the kitchen, talking to her cook, Tunzen. "If only I could have had him just a little longer," she said.

I put Willy's last letters in a blue file folder and find myself wishing there were more. These last letters especially have made me feel close to him. On November 22 Melly wrote to Walter and Lore in Shanghai. "I can't reconcile myself to the fact that he wasn't granted at least a few years in retirement and peace — that we couldn't spend our old age together in our small house." I think about how free Willy felt at the end of his life. If he had lived, how would that feeling have affected us all?

In Bremen, Melly continued to receive mail from Willy. His last parcel arrived on February 7, 1948, when he had been dead four months. It was a package of airmail paper, very carefully packed. She wrote to Lore and Walter, "I was moved to tears."

After my grandfather died, my grandmother's letters were no longer placed in the blue binder. They were kept, but not in such an orderly fashion. After arranging them according to the dates on which they were written, my mother and I continue to read. We arrive at a letter my grandmother wrote at the end of January 1950. Melly was describing a discussion with a municipal official concerning some repairs to her house. The official turned out to be a former employee at the Ag. Weser shipyard. He told Melly that he had worked very well together with my grandfather for fourteen years, that Herr Frensdorff was "the most decent, the pleasantest boss in the whole world." And then, Melly wrote, "We both began to sob a little."

"I soon start crying," says my mother. Her voice develops a catch, but she laughs.

I laugh also. "Me too," I say, realizing that my eyes are wet.

Melly
Frensdorff
in Vienna
about 1900

Unbroken Links

Talia is eating Froot Loops, pastel-coloured cereal with a cloying smell of artificial flavouring. It is a Saturday morning in late spring.

"Tell me," she says, with the spoon poised to go in her mouth, "the story of me being born."

I always begin the same way. "It was late September, and you were big enough to be born. Daddy drove to the hospital."

"And you stuck out way out." She stretches her hand in front of her as far as she can reach. "You were fat."

"I was not *fat*," I protest.

"You were, you were. You were so big you couldn't get into the car. You had to ride on top. There was a special seat belt on the roof that held you on."

Smiling, I say, "The next morning, they got me ready."
As I explain the procedures that a Caesarean birth involves,
Talia looks at me intently. "Then Daddy came into the oper-
ating room. He had to wear a coat and a cap over his head.
When they pulled you out, Daddy said, 'It's a girl!'"

"He should have said, '*She's* a girl!'"

I lapse into silence. But Talia does not let me end the
story there. "You forgot something — about me being the bath
demonstration baby!"

And so I tell her again about how slippery babies are, how
difficult they are to bathe and how the nurses show new
mothers what to do. One had asked me if she might use Talia.

"Why did they pick me?"

"Well, maybe it was because I was a second-time mother. I wouldn't get so nervous." She doesn't like this answer.
She frowns. "Maybe it was because they could see that you
were a calm baby. You wouldn't get upset and cry your head
off."

Talia nods. The story is hers. And I let her have it. Since I
have recently been writing about how *I* was born, I am interested to see how Talia moulds a similar narrative. What
events does she want to emphasize? And what do I choose to
accentuate? How do we construct these stories?

In early May, 1948, in Bremen, the weather was unsea-
sonably hot. The fruit trees in the garden behind the house
on Weyerbergstrasse were all in blossom. But they made
Melly sad. "Actually Daddy should have arrived by now," she
wrote to her daughter. "I can't express how much sorrow I
feel as I look down into the flowering garden....How sense-
less everything has become since I know that he won't be
coming home."

One day she visited Vegesack, on the Weser River, to
watch the sailing boats. They were a pretty sight, tacking

back and forth briskly across the water. But they reminded her that Willy was dead. "It is totally, totally incomprehensible that this and everything else should go on the same way even though he has been taken away forever. It amazes me that I am still here."

Shanghai was also warm, but not yet stifling. Lore and Walter took advantage of the temperate weather to visit the ancient city of Wuxi on Tai Lake, west of Shanghai. They travelled at a leisurely pace in a newly purchased Dodge, their chauffeur at the wheel.

Tunzen, the cook, also accompanied them. Although in his late twenties, he had travelled little, and every morning he rose early to admire the scenery. He told my mother he had never seen mountains before. In one of our photo albums, a picture of Tunzen and the chauffeur is pasted beside the dried sprig of edelweiss my father had with him when he fled Austria. They stand in front of the Dodge. The chauffeur, a short man, is wearing a rumpled three-piece suit, a white shirt and a tie. Tunzen, who is taller and rather aristocratic, wears a striped Chinese jacket and baggy pants.

In Manchuria, the Communists were laying seige to several Nationalist strongholds — Changchum, Mukden and Chinchow. At Tai Lake, Lore and Walter took a boat tour and watched the drifting mists for which the lake is famous.

Towards the end of May, Melly began to worry about Lore and Walter because she had received no letter for three weeks. Then, in June, her anxiety was suddenly dispelled. My parents told her that Lore was pregnant. "Children, children, such joy that you want to make me a grandmother!" she glowed. "We will be four, and the gap that our unforgettable one left is closing again. That's the way of the world. The links should not break." She didn't care whether the child was a boy or a girl. "That one must leave to fate." And she approved of my parents' ideas for names. "I like Claudia or Claudienna as well as Hans Stefen."

Two weeks later, in another letter, my grandmother reminisced about being pregnant. "In the middle of a deep sleep, fists and feet would twitch." As my mother reads, I too begin to think back. I am vividly recollecting those substantial kicks that caused my belly to surge visibly when I hear the words, "Just don't forget the name Thomas would be especially nice." My mother puts the letter down and looks at me.

When our son exited my womb at 1:30 P.M. on October 16, 1985, Gordon and I had not decided what to call him. We wanted to see what the baby looked like first. We stared at his downy head and peered into his luminous dark eyes. Gordon sat in an armchair at the foot of my hospital bed, reading names out of a book. In my diary is the sheet of paper on which he wrote seventeen names – our shortlist.

We left the hospital on a windy morning hung with dark clouds. Our son was still just Baby Cornwall. When he was a week old we had a birthday party to mark the anniversary. There was a banana cake and one candle. We had not yet settled on a name.

Another two days went by before we reached a decision: he would be Thomas. "I would not have expected to call him Thomas, but the name evolved and seemed to suit him," I explained in my diary. I had no idea until now that it was a favourite of my grandmother's.

On October 20, 1948, Melly was able to dispatch mail by air for the first time in nine years. "I hope that this letter will be in your hands in seven days," she wrote to my parents. "Then Claudia, or Thomas, or both, will surely be visible."

While tucking my son into bed one night, I tell him about the letters. "She thought that my mom might have twins – a boy and a girl. There weren't twins, but it turned out she was right anyway. Both Thomas and Claudia became visible. Isn't that funny?"

Thomas is less impressed by the coincidence than I am. He is sleepy. "I guess it's in the genes," he mutters before closing his eyes and turning away from me.

I was born in Shanghai's Da Hwa Hospital on October 27, 1948, two weeks late. "You took your time," my mother used to say. I always took pride in the fact, as if it were something I had chosen.

My grandmother relayed her congratulations the next day. "It [the baby] was obviously sent by our unforgettable daddy. Therefore, it will certainly be a first-rate girl just like her mother. Now I will go out and find a bottle of cherry brandy with which I can toast Claudia properly....Can I buy something for Claudia? There are balloons again, and pacifiers....So, my dears, I can't find the right words to express my deep happiness. It is too nice and a blessing of heaven that I was allowed to experience this day."

Reading Melly's letter almost makes me feel like raising a glass myself, so infectious is her happiness. I am startled at how much pleasure her pleasure gives me. The words, buried for years in my parents' trunk, still sing. She had a gift for happiness, I realize now. I had seen it before in her letters, although I wasn't aware of it when she was alive.

I find it hard to reconcile the woman I knew with the woman whose letters I have been reading. I lean Melly's old family photographs against my computer so that I can look at them while I write. On the left, I put her father, Joseph Marholz. He wears a fedora, a white wing-collar shirt, a suit and a coat draped over his left shoulder. He is bearded, and his eyes, which I know were blue, seem very light in colour. He apprenticed as a house painter, specializing in decorations. Later, he built houses and sold them. He collected paintings and loved opera. On holidays in the country, he would fling open the shuttered windows of his room and sing arias to the green hills.

Next to him, I put my grandmother, Melly, at age two, wearing a white eyelet dress and high-buttoned boots. Her mother, Anna, a slim woman in a dark printed dress with a dark lace collar, is holding her hand. The two look very earnestly at the camera. At three, Melly is photographed with her older sister, Henrietta. Both are wearing white lace dresses and tartan sashes. Henrietta holds a watering can, Melly a hoop. My grandmother has a very pronounced pout. There is a stump behind them and a trough made of a hollow log in front. But they are not outdoors. This is a scene constructed in the photographer's studio, Pokorny's Comfort Atelier.

At about thirteen, Melly stands behind a small ornate table on which several books and a sheaf of papers are arranged. She wears a white lace blouse, a dark skirt and a dotted scarf knotted around her neck like a tie. On the back of the photograph, in her handwriting, are the words, "*Per ardua ad astra!*"

Around this time, Anna Marholz, who already had a third child, a daughter Ophelia, gave birth to a fourth. Her labour did not go well. There were screams from the bedroom. And bloody cloths and bloody sheets. When it was all over, my grandmother had a new sister, Anita. But her mother was dead.

Two years later, Melly's father married again. His new wife was Hedwig von Klingsborg, a young, beautiful Czech woman. Melly decided to leave Vienna and go to her stepmother's sister, Flora, who lived in Trieste. In this sun-washed port on the Adriatic, then part of the Austro-Hungarian Empire, Melly learned Italian and worked as a bookkeeper for Gebrüder Weiss, an oil exporting firm. In Trieste, Melly had her photograph taken in a studio at Piazza della Borsa 7. She wears a long white skirt, a tucked vest and a lace blouse. Her waist is small and her skin flawless. Her dark hair is thick and curly under a broad-brimmed black hat trimmed with black-and-white ostrich feathers. In her right hand, she holds flowers, in her left a parasol. She is very pretty. Is this how she looked on Sunday, April 9, 1911, the day she met Willy Frensdorff at an open-air concert in Trieste? Did he see her gift for joy under the broad-brimmed hat? The gift that I did not see until much later?

Melly joined us in Canada when I was thirteen. By this time, my mother had told me that Anna had died in childbirth when Melly herself was thirteen. I knew too that she had left home soon after her father remarried. The story impressed me, and I thought that perhaps it could help me to understand my grandmother's sadness. I wondered if her melancholy was somehow connected with grief over her mother. As if she had never really got over it.

Now I wonder how much of her unhappiness was related to grief over Willy. On September 7, 1947, he had written, "After all, the Nazis were not smart enough to destroy us!" Three weeks later he was dead. Perhaps it seemed to Melly that they did get him in the end.

How would my relationship with my grandmother have been different if I had heard Willy's story when I was younger? What if Melly had told me what she had told my mother when *she* was thirteen, on that day in 1933?

Nationalist $100 bill, 1949

17

Violent Fluctuations

A beautiful Indian summer embraced Shanghai during the fall of 1948. The languorous sunny days and cool nights made the civil war in the north seem very far away. But by the beginning of November the Communists had seized all of Manchuria. Two of their armies, totalling half a million men, began marching towards Hsuchow, a key city strategically located in the Yangtze delta north of Nanking.

In Shanghai, the inflation spiralled crazily upwards. No one knew how to stop it. In August 1948, Chiang Kai-shek had directed his son, General Chiang Ching-kuo, to take charge of the city's economy. He froze wages, prices and foreign exchange and arrested currency speculators, but at the end of October, he resigned. Prices went higher than ever.

The cost of rice tripled overnight. Borrowers were willing to pay anything from 90 to 300 per cent interest a month, confident that the rise in commodity prices would offset these usurious rates. "Many small and middle class people," my father wrote in an article in the *North China Daily News*, "seem to think that a few rice bags represent a greater measure of security than the possession of paper notes whose value is subject to violent fluctuations."

In my desk drawer are Gold Yuan bills, dated 1949, mostly in denominations of 100. I found them among my parents' papers, folded and tucked into a couple of airmail envelopes. Printed on the 100s in red ink is a steamer docked along a wharf beside the Bund, its smokestack billowing. I can see the British Consulate near the Garden Bridge, the Cathay Hotel with its distinctive spire. The water on the Whangpoo is flat. A sampan floats in the foreground. The notes are very crisp. On one of them, my father scribbled names and phone numbers.

Thomas counts them for me. "Four thousand eight hundred, four thousand nine hundred, five thousand...there are more than five thousand dollars! What are they worth?"

"Not much," I tell him. He looks at me dubiously.

To meet the weekly payroll for her business, Lore needed a duffle bag full of these dollars. On payday, her tailors ran to buy their rice, since an hour's delay substantially reduced their purchasing power. At the same time, my father was hiding illegal American dollars behind the light sockets and exchanging them for Yuan bills on the black market. "Once I was cheated," he says. "I brought home a bag of money and found that under the layer of Chinese notes, the trader had placed even more worthless newspaper cut like the dollars."

In December, Lore wrote her mother to say that she and Walter were thinking of moving to Bremen. She wondered if they could obtain a German visa. When Tientsin fell to the

Communists early in 1949, my Uncle Günther was convinced political and economic stability would never be restored. He left for Europe on board a Greek ship, the *Captain Marcos.*

But on January 22, Chiang Kai-shek handed power over to Vice President Li Tsung-jen. Many people were hopeful that the new leader would stop the fighting. Walter and Lore decided not to return to Bremen after all. For $800 U.S., they purchased a long lease on a bungalow in Hungjao, the rural suburb where my father had first tried horseback riding before the war.

Surrounded by graceful leafy trees, their house hugged the ground. Frogs lived in the grassy shallows of the pond in front. Birds nested nearby. The place had only one problem: it was a little small. As was customary for Europeans in Shanghai, the Wieners employed several servants. In addition to Tunzen and his wife, they also had their chauffeur and a nanny for me, Ah King. To accommodate everyone, they added one more room.

At home, I have a thick pile of the columns, now yellowed and brittle, that my father wrote for the financial pages of the *Daily News.* However, for the front-page stories I have to visit the sixth floor of the University of British Columbia Main Library. The newspaper is on microform. I feed the film through a special machine and look at it on a screen. Watching the pages scroll past reminds me of trying to read while riding in a car. I feel queasy. I wheeze from the dust in the air.

In general terms, the story is a familiar one: the relentless progress of the People's Liberation Army, the incompetence and corruption of the Nationalists. I think what surprises me is how long Walter and Lore stayed. But I can understand their reluctance to leave. Shanghai had provided a refuge at a time when no other place did. It was the needle in the haystack. Chaotic though the city was, it represented security.

Shortly after Li Tsung-jen replaced Chiang Kai-shek, the Communists took Peking, meeting only token resistence. Mao Tse-tung moved into a Ming dynasty pavilion in a quiet corner of the Forbidden City.

To the south, along the Yangtze River, the People's Liberation Army was preparing a flotilla of boats to ferry more than a million men across. Peace talks between the Nationalists and the Communists dragged on fruitlessly. Every day, Walter read the dispatches that arrived at the newspaper. Did he think that the Nationalists would somehow manage to keep the Communists away from Shanghai, I wonder? Or did he believe that Shanghai would accommodate itself to the new ideology?

"*Maskee!*" said the Shanghainese. "Never mind! No problem!" It expressed an irrepressible optimism, a thumbing of the nose at circumstances. Had a typhoon spilled a foot of water on the streets? Maskee! Did a pound of rice cost $1500? Maskee! Had undisciplined Nationalist soldiers robbed you and would the municipal police do nothing about it? Maskee! Did it seem to Walter that this polyglot and sophisticated city that had endured so much could endure anything?

In 1952, he would write to a friend, John Ahlers: "Well, after you left [Shanghai], I carried on for a while although the clouds were gathering fast for all kinds of people who could read the writings on the wall. However, there were the old China hands, the British Consul among them, who assured me that the Chinese after all were Chinese and that they had absorbed so many cultures and so on and so forth. As you know, all this balderdash was not worth a dime, or a penny rather."

In Bremen, my grandmother was uneasy about the Chinese political situation. Nevertheless, she was delighted to learn that my parents had found a new and larger home. "In Hungjao perhaps the university district — very green in the Yangtze district? And you have a garden terrace? Oh, how wonderful! And can you eat outside? And are there primroses, pansies and other small flowers? And who works in the garden? The chauffeur?"

In April, Lore's Uncle Kurt, who was living in Halle, East Germany, wrote to say that he was painting murals for the government. One was in an orphanage, another in the dining room of the local Hall of Socialism. My grandmother had told him about the Wieners' move, and he imagined them on the other side of the globe, leading an elegant and luxurious existence. "Perhaps even now, your minds at peace, you are sitting in your beautiful new bungalow and feeding goldfish with ants while here I harbour frightful notions. What do you think happens when I let fall the remark that I have real 'Chinese' as relatives, that you sit on small islands overgrown with lotus plants, sip rice wine out of jade green cups and hold long conversations about the virtuous insights in the Tao-te-ching?"

Once again, the Wieners were thinking about leaving. On April 12, Walter obtained a visa to enter Switzerland, and on April 13, a visa for France. The permits were stamped into the new passport the Austrian consul in Shanghai had issued him. However, these were short-term solutions only: he could stay two months in Switzerland, five days in France.

In the U.B.C. library, as I read about the last months of Nationalist rule in China, it is quiet. Exams are over and there are very few students here. I scan the headlines, hearing muffled footsteps occasionally.

APRIL 21. TWO BRITISH WARSHIPS ATTACKED IN YANGTZE — 17 DEAD, 20 WOUNDED

On April 23, Communist soldiers crossed China's principal waterway in every kind of craft they could lay their hands upon: junks, sampans, fishing boats, even bamboo rafts. Then they marched into Nanking, the erstwhile Nationalist capital.

APRIL 25. SHANGHAI TENSELY AWAITS APPROACH OF RED ARMIES

But the armies didn't come just yet. They surprised everyone by halting for several days. Mao's troops had travelled over a thousand miles in a year. He wanted to give them a rest and lost no significant military advantage by waiting.

In Shanghai, the Nationalists proclaimed martial law. Walter had a press pass to get him through the checkpoints, but living on the outskirts of the city made Lore and Walter nervous. When friends of theirs, the Müllers, who lived on Route Ghisei in the French Concession, told them of an empty house nearby, at Number 192, they moved in. The Kuomintang were still full of assurances that they would do their utmost to hang on.

MAY 3. NATIONALISTS TO DEFEND SHANGHAI TO BITTER END

But Walter was not convinced. On May 3, he applied for yet another visa – this time from the government of Canada. It was the third visitor's visa stamped into his passport. He had permission to stay three months.

The Communists were drawing closer and closer. They were infiltrating the Nationalist positions just north of Hungjao airport and fiercely attacking the town of Chwansha east of the city. On the financial pages of the *Daily News*, Walter continued to observe economic developments. An

American dollar was fetching 8,000,000 Gold Yuan notes on the open market and a Chinese silver dollar traded at 3,500,000 Yuan. Interest rates had skyrocketed to 600 per cent a month. "The problems of local firms concerning feasible methods of wage and salary payments were still unsolved yesterday," my father wrote. How could he seem so calm?

MAY 18. RED ARMIES ENCIRCLING SHANGHAI

To the north, where the Whangpoo River met the Yangtze, the Kuomintang forces were desperately trying to prevent the Communists from shutting their gateway to the sea. In the south, the Liberation Armies were just ten kilometres away from Shanghai, marching along the Hangchow railway line.

MAY 23. HUNGJAO GOLF COURSE NOW BATTLEFIELD

The golfers were gone. No one was knocking a ball down the fairway. Instead, the Nationalist artillery was pounding the Communists, who had advanced from their positions around the airport the previous night. The *Daily News* reported that when a German family living near the west end of the Avenue Joffre phoned a friend living in Hungjao district to ask him how far away the Communists were, he replied, "They're right here in my house, drinking water."

The east bank of the Whangpoo River, opposite the Bund, the commercial centre of Shanghai, was the scene of another bloody battle. Thousands of Chinese and foreigners crowded onto the rooftops of downtown buildings to see the fighting barely a kilometre away. Explosions rocked office buildings and rifle fire crackled throughout the night.

Unaccountably, the Kuomintang held a victory parade on

May 24. As a procession of trucks carrying battle-weary veterans wound its way through the streets, 100,000 people watched. The Nationalists maintained they were successfully holding the Communist forces across the river at bay.

But on May 25, Walter was roused by his cook. "Master," said Tunzen, "Gong Chan Dang are here." My father looked out of the window and saw a barricade in the street. Two soldiers in green uniforms were manning it, their crossed bayonets gleaming in the morning light. For the third time in his life, my father had woken up to find himself under military occupation.

*Claudia
Wiener and
Ah King,
Shanghai,
June 1949*

18

Who Will Take Care of You?

"We knew we had to get out," says my mother now.

There was no future for the Wieners in Shanghai. Not only was Walter's opposition to Communism strong, it was well documented. Anyone reading the paper could see it. An article of his about currency reform in Russia had even aroused a rebuke from someone called I. Grodko, a lecturer at the Moscow Institute of Finance. The *Daily News* had printed Grodko's letter on January 31, 1948: "These assertions are factually inaccurate and likewise are the fruits of a big theoretical misunderstanding."

But the early days of the new regime brought an unforeseen respite. Life carried on. The *North China Daily News* continued to publish: soldiers did not lock its doors. In my mother's business on Avenue Pétain, the tailors still cut and sewed.

On June 17, under the headline "Est modus in rebus," Walter Wiener wrote, "No one expected the authorities to create a millenium a few days after they started cleansing the local financial and economic Augean stables." But he was surprised by the "splendid behaviour of troops and military personnel in general which shows a striking contrast to the past." He mentioned an incident in which a number of Shanghailanders drove out to Hungjao to check on their bungalows. When they were stopped by sentries, they thought, "Ah, just the old game again." But the Communists did not demand any money as the Nationalist soldiers had so often done in the past. They were polite and explained that the area was not considered quite safe by the authorities. Walter was also favourably impressed by the government policies concerning foreign currency and gold and silver bars. He concluded the piece by writing, "The prospects of a speedy return to normality seem to brighten."

Photographs labelled "June 1949" show my father in a holiday mood, smiling, standing beside my mother, who is holding me. I have a thin crown of blonde hair and I am wearing a light-coloured dress. I look at my father very seriously. In another photograph, I am standing in a large playpen holding on to the upper bar. My nanny, Ah King, a plump, round-faced woman, crouches beside me and peers through the bars. She and I are both laughing.

But there was no speedy return to normality. The Communists were intent on substantial changes. Soon even the *North China Daily News*, with its slogan "Impartial Not Neutral" proudly displayed under the masthead, was affected. On June 25, the editor, R. T. Peyton-Griffin, was forced to retract a story about the Nationalists disrupting shipping by laying mines in an estuary of the Yangtze River. He wrote a letter to the Shanghai Military Control Commission of the

Chinese People's Liberation Army. He tendered his "sincere and humble apology" for the story that had appeared on June 10. He assured the commission that he would do "whatever is necessary to ensure that there shall be no repetition of such a mistake in the future." And he reprinted the letter on the front page of the paper.

"Friends got an exit visa for me," my father explains, when I ask how he and my mother got out of Shanghai. "They said I was a worker at the *North China Daily News*."

"Were there difficulties?"

"I don't recall."

My father was lucky. In *The Fall of Shanghai*, Noel Barber writes about several people who waited months, even years, for their permits to come through. To obtain her exit visa, my mother had to give a prescribed amount of severance pay to her tailors. A slip of paper in my parents' trunk is proof that she did. In my father's writing, the note says, "Sept. 21, 1949. This is to certify that we received our pay-off money from Mrs. Lore Maria Wiener in full settlement of our claims against her." Below this are four signatures in Chinese. Considering its importance, the document seems remarkably informal — a few handwritten words unadorned by any official seals or stamps.

"And just when we had arranged everything, we almost lost all our papers," says my father. Half an hour after leaving the office of a Chinese accountant who was helping them to prepare their documents, Walter and Lore realized that they had left their papers, passports and money behind. "We roared back in a rickshaw. The accountant had gone home and the office was in the process of being cleaned by a servant. But the papers were still there on his desk. It was a tense half hour."

Tunzen agreed to take care of the dog, Jackie, and the cat, Tommy. My parents gave him their last gold bar.

"Who is going to take care of you?" Tunzen asked them.

Lore and Walter had booked a passage on the *General Gordon* – first class for my mother and me, third class for my father. When the Wieners took a taxi to the Shanghai and Hongkew Wharf at 610 Tungtaming Road, Tunzen and Ah King accompanied them. Ah King held me during the ride and at the gangplank handed me to my mother.

"Then it started," my mother says. "You began to sob. You sobbed so much that you were hiccupping uncontrollably. I think it lasted all day." Ah King had taken care of me ever since I was a couple of months old. We shared a bedroom and if I cried in the night, she rocked me back to sleep. When I began to eat solid foods, Ah King fed me rice with a large spoon.

"You'll see," she told my mother, "this child will always be a good eater."

"I never worried about you," I say to my kids. "I wasn't fussy and I knew you wouldn't be either. It's all because of Ah King." Of course, I don't really know whether it is. But I like to think so. That in itself makes a kind of connection.

"Ah King," says Thomas slowly. "I like that name."

In the U.B.C. library, I come across a book of photographs by Sam Tata called *Shanghai – 1949: The End of an Era.* I am leafing through it casually when suddenly I stop, transfixed by one of the images. It is titled, "Nuns Leaving Shanghai before May from Shanghai & Hongkew Wharf." The nuns are walking up the same gangplank on which I wept so inconsolably. A sign along the side of gangplank says in large letters, "The President Lines." This was the shipping company to which the *General Gordon* belonged. The picture does not show the bottom of the gangplank or the top where it meets the ship. The black-robed nuns are suspended against the sky.

Tata shot the photograph for its symbolic value; the nuns' faces are hidden by their wimples. I don't know their ages or have any sense of them as individuals. "The Europeans are going" is what the picture means. Still, there are some details, like the way the sign is lashed onto the gangplank, the way the fingers of the nuns' right hands curl over the railing, the way they stoop as they walk up the incline.

I don't remember sobbing as I left Shanghai. Before I saw Tata's book, the scene existed only in my imagination. I put in what my mother had told me about it: the noise of my wailing, my despair at being separated from Ah King. It did not contain much in the way of visual details. Now I picture my mother leaning at the same angle as the nuns, one of her hands curving around the railing.

The *General Gordon* sailed out of Shanghai on Sunday, September 25, 1949. It was 3:50 A.M. My parents were asleep. They did not lean over the deck rail and see the *North China Daily News* building recede into the distance or watch as the Garden Bridge, where they had so often walked under the eyes of a Japanese sentry, grew gradually smaller. Next morning, they were in the East China Sea, heading south.

I find one letter from this time, written by my mother, in pencil, on yellow paper — a first draft.

"Sept. 49. Dear Müllers: We are in the middle of our adventure. The trip on the *Gordon* was really not so nice. First class was all right but third class — awful holes deep in the ship's hold. However, it was not as bad as the Burkhardts described because my husband was able to stay in the first class during the day....Puki was not as troublesome on the ship as we expected especially as she ate everything, soup, meat, vegetables, as it came. The child care was excellent."

The *General Gordon* stopped briefly in Hong Kong and Japan. The last my parents saw of Asia was the dock in Yokohama, where Japanese students came aboard to sing songs of farewell.

One November night in 1992 I have a bad dream. My husband and I, my mother-in-law, Charlotte Cornwall, and about twenty other people are in a cabin in the mountains. Sometimes they seem to be the Kootenays and sometimes the Himalayas. Across the valley I can see another cabin known as the Sailor's Hut. Although it is far away, I can see it very well.

Somehow we receive a warning that the Chinese will drop a bomb on the hut across the valley. I run inside our cabin and cover my face with my hands. Nevertheless, I still see the explosion — the mushroom cloud. When the dust and clouds subside, my cabin mates and I get up. We are not injured, but we wonder what to do about the radiation. Should we drive away? We don't think this is a good idea because there is a dirt road and we believe that the dust might be especially radioactive there. We consider washing the floor, forgetting about the possibility of radioactivity in the water. I wonder when we will begin to experience symptoms. I don't seem to have children, and I fear that I will be unable to have them now because of my exposure. The dream is very visual. Much later I will still recall the cabin with its dark polished wooden floors and varnished log walls, its small windows, the bright green leaves outside in the streaming sunshine.

In my diary I write, "I wake up and with relief realize it was all a dream. The anxiety slowly ebbs out of my body. I remember that just before falling asleep the previous night, I had been reading *The Fall of Shanghai*. I was particularly horrified by Barber's account of how the Communists took Nationalist strongholds in the interior after long seiges. People were starving — wearing the skins of cats and dogs that they had eaten. These events were taking place just a couple of months before I was born. "Is this where this feeling of sick fear — of the destruction of everything — came from?" I asked in my diary.

Christmas, 1992. After dinner, my father retires early. He is having one of his bad days. My mother says, "He's anxious, thinks there's a revolution going on outside, thinks that he won't be able to get his money out of the bank. I told him, 'If there really were a revolution going on, I'd be running around like crazy. I'd be excited. Trust me.'

"He said, 'Why should I?' and shrugged."

*The Wiener
family,
Vancouver,
about 1953*

19

A Deportation Order

October 16, 1949. When the Wieners alighted from the train
in Vancouver's CN Station on Main Street, they could see the
North Shore mountains beyond the railyards. The peaks were
lightly dusted with snow, but it was mild.

They had been travelling for three weeks. After the *General Gordon* docked in San Francisco, they had immediately
boarded a Great Northern Railroad train and headed for
Canada. They travelled in bond, which meant that they could
not leave the train at any of the stations. American officials
imposed the restriction because Walter Wiener had applied
for a visa to enter the United States some years before. They
thought he might now try to get into the country illegally.

On the lawn in front of the station, derelict men were
sleeping. Lore was shocked. In all the years she had spent in

China she had never seen white people lying on the ground. What kind of country was this, she wondered.

The family registered at the Ivanhoe Hotel just a block away from the station. The district was so run-down and seedy that Walter was frightened. "You can't walk alone here," he told Lore.

A few days later, the family moved from the Ivanhoe to the Buchan Hotel on Haro Street. But the couple and their child didn't stay there for very long, either. In a letter to a Shanghai friend, Walter explained, "One nice day I found myself with my baby daughter and wife on the streets. We had been given notice in our hotel on account of the baby (it is extremely difficult to get rooms or apartments that will take babies, which seem to constitute something of a criminal offence here whether born in or out of wedlock)."

In a restaurant, Walter and Lore fell into conversation with an elderly couple, the Everetts. After my parents had told their story, the couple said, "You can stay with us. We have space." Later, my father would describe the Everetts' kindness as "a sheer miracle."

Monday, January 16, 1950, 2:10 P.M., Dominion Immigration Building, Vancouver, British Columbia. The building, which would be demolished in 1976, lay between Thurlow and Burrard on Hastings Street. G. W. Douglas, J. L. Ross and A. F. Watts, members of a board of inquiry, were meeting on this cold and snowy afternoon in order to interview Walter and Lore Wiener. The Wieners' three-month visitor's visa had expired, and they had applied to remain in Canada.

I find the minutes of the hearing in my parents' black chest. They are typed on eleven pages of legal-sized beige paper. At the top of the first page, I see that the case had been assigned file number 100009. Mr. Douglas, the chairman of the board, began the examination by questioning my father.

Q. "Of what country are you a citizen at the present time?"

A. "I have an Austrian passport."

Q. "Do you claim to be a citizen of Austria?"

A. "I am a citizen of Austria."

Q. "By what right do you claim to be a citizen of Austria?"

A. "Well, I was born there. My father was also Austrian."

Q. "What is your racial origin on your father's side?"

A. "Well, my father and mother were of the Jewish religion and I became a Christian in 1938 in Vienna."

Q. "I understand then that you are of the Jewish race?"

A. "Yes, if there is anything like that."

Q. "You presume your father to be deceased?"

A. "Yes."

Q. "The same information would then apply to your mother as you have given regarding your father?"

A. "Yes."

Walter explained to the board that an Austrian lawyer who had made inquiries for him about his parents had not been able to find any trace of them. He mentioned that his brother, who had returned to Austria the year before, had not discovered anything either.

Douglas wanted to know whether Walter had been deported from any country and whether he had ever been in trouble with the police or charged with a criminal offence. He had questions about Walter's assets both inside and outside Canada.

Q. "What is the amount of money that you have in Canada at the present time in cash?"

A. "Around $100."

Douglas also wanted to know whether Walter Wiener had been able to find a job. My father's search for work had been frustrating. From a letter he wrote to John Ahlers about his first few years in Canada, I know that he worked briefly for the *Vancouver Sun*. He described it as "a very American-ized affair where people gave me to understand that I was not up to their standards especially since I did not observe the union rules." He told John that he received "the stereotyped answer everywhere; too old, too old for the junior staff, too young for the senior staff and so forth and so on. I contacted the University where one professor handed me on to the other people like a hot potato."

But one lucky stroke was that on January 14, two days before the hearing in the Immigration Building, the *B.C. Financial and Industrial Times* had published an article of Walter's called "The China I Left." He was able to show the board a letter from the magazine's editor, Walter Dent, which stated that Walter Wiener had a permanent contract as a space writer with the publication. The letter is labelled "Exhibit A."

Then G. W. Douglas called upon Lore Wiener.

Q. "Have all the questions that your husband has been asked been answered truthfully to the best of your knowledge?"
A. "Yes."
Q. "Of what country do you claim to be a citizen?"
A. "Austria."
Q. "By what right do you claim that?"
A. "I am married to an Austrian. I have the same citizenship as my husband."

At this point in the questioning, A. F. Watts wanted to know about Lore Wiener's racial origin. She told him that her father was of Jewish extraction but a member of the Protestant Church in Germany, and that he had left the country of his birth in 1939 and gone to Shanghai as a refugee.

J. L. Ross, whose title is given as secretary of the board, wanted to know about Lore's medical history. My mother reported that she had no physical defects and that there had been no insanity in her family.

Attached to the transcript of the hearing are Exhibits A to J. They are mostly letters from colleagues of Walter in Shanghai that attest to my father's expertise in economic matters. The Dean of the Cathedral there and the Dean of Christ Church Cathedral in Vancouver also wrote on his behalf.

Mr. Ross moved "that Walter Wiener's application to land and remain in Canada be rejected and his detention and deportation be ordered under Section 33 of the Immigration Act and Regulations, to the country of his birth or citizenship or to the country whence he came in that he is unable to comply with the following Orders in Council: P.C. 2743 dated at Ottawa, Canada, June 2, 1949, in that he is not included in the admissible classes as outlined in the said Order in Council; P.C. 2744, in that he is not in possession of a proper Immigrant Visa."

The chairman declared the motion unanimous and issued a deportation order. He explained, however, that Walter Wiener had the right to appeal.

Q. "Do you wish to appeal?"
A. "Yes I do."

Douglas also issued a bond for conditional release. This meant that Walter Wiener was not detained but was required to report in person to G. W. Douglas between 10:00 A.M. and noon on the first day of each month. If he failed to do this, or if he failed to "surrender himself to an Immigration Officer when called upon to do so," he would owe fifty dollars to "our Sovereign Lord the King."

On February 9, Walter received a letter from the minister of citizenship and immigration stating, "The said appeals have been dismissed by the Honourable, the Minister of Citizenship and Immigration. However, it has been further decided that you may be granted an extension of temporary stay in this country to December 31st, 1950."

Walter and Lore decided to take advantage of this temporary stay. They believed that if they somehow managed to establish themselves, the problems about their visa would be resolved. But how were they to do this? The arrangement with the *B.C. Financial and Industrial Times* did not turn out to be permanent. Walter did not publish another article there.

However, finally he succeeded in persuading some "financial people" to lend him $2100 to start a business. His letter to John Ahlers recounts, "I got a loan without securities — a thing unheard of in Vancouver where every dime is being looked upon and then quietly pocketed again." In March, Walter and Lore found a small shop in a good location on the west side of Vancouver. There was no money to rent an apartment as well, so they lived in the back. "Then our adventure actually started. There were no workers, no helpers, no nothing so to speak, and my wife had to work 18 hours a day to sell, cut, sew and design clothes. Our financial helpers moreover expected something like an oil bonanza from our little establishment. They told us to order stock from the biggest Scottish firms, and when the bills came around they just politely shrugged their shoulders and told me that bills of course have to be paid and there I was."

Among my parents' documents, I find some correspondence between my father and a senator named Gray Turgeon. In April, my father informed Turgeon that the shop's sales for February had totalled $95, and for March, $180.

"Someone suggested we contact this man," my mother tells me when I ask. "Now I don't remember who gave us the idea. Your daddy was always good at finding out things like that. I don't know any more what he did for us, either." From the *Parliamentary Index for 1950*, I learn that the senator was a member of the Liberal Party, that he had represented the Cariboo in the House of Commons and been appointed to the Senate in 1947.

In June, Gray Turgeon responded to my father's report. "I feel fairly well satisfied that when the matter is again under review at the end of this year, you will be admitted permanently to Canada....I feel certain that your own situation will improve between now and the end of the year because of the conduct of Mrs. Wiener's business." Sales in April and May increased to $654 and $937. The business began to employ five women, one as an apprentice.

The senator turned out to be right. The deportation order was revoked and the Wieners were permitted to stay. On September 11, 1952, they officially declared their intention to become citizens. On January 12, 1956, they paid a twenty-two-dollar naturalization fee. Four months later, they received a letter from the minister of citizenship and immigration, Jack Pickersgill: "I extend to you a warm welcome on this solemn occasion and I invite you to share with us the ancient liberties of a free people living together in harmony, under a democratic Government which recognizes the rights of all its citizens." On May 31, the process was finished. The Wieners renounced their Austrian nationality and became Canadians.

My father's journey had begun on an overcast day in October in Vienna's Sudbahnhof eighteen years before. My mother's had started sixteen years earlier in late May, in Bremen's main railway station. They had lived through a war and a revolution; they had travelled three quarters of the way around the globe.

After renting the shop on West Boulevard in Vancouver, the Wieners would never move very far away again. They changed the location of their business two more times, on both occasions setting up no more than a kilometre from the original premises. They eventually bought a house. But it, too, was close by, about a block from their first store. The Wieners' journey was over.

Now, thinking back to my childhood, I am surprised that I had no awareness of the trauma my parents had undergone. I noticed things, but I didn't understand them. For instance, that knocking on our front door. I don't remember when it started. I was maybe nine or ten. It was spring, I think. We heard a rapping. One of us went to answer it. No one was there. Later that day or perhaps the next, it happened again. And then again and again. My father grew angry. He would race to the door at the sound. Finally he saw the teen-agers. They had ducktail haircuts and wore blakies on their black leather boots. They laughed. The angrier my father was, the more they laughed. I remember that, in an attempt to identify the youths, he visited the local high school, Point Grey Junior High. He went from classroom to classroom, looking at the boys. I don't know whether his visit to the school paid off or whether the teen-agers grew tired of the game. However, the knocking stopped. But I remember that I was embarrassed. I thought he was overreacting to a childish prank.

Now I understand him better. I think of what he has told me about Vienna after Anschluss: "You never knew whether a knock on the door was a friend or the Gestapo. It was touch and go."

Launching the Scharnhorst *in Bremen, December 1934.*
Franz Stapelfeldt, in cap, stands beside Hitler.

20

Facing Your Fears

January 10, 1993. A letter arrives in the mail for me. "It is my pleasure," writes someone called Helen Eriks, "to advise you that the Canada Council is offering you a grant of $3,673 for your project." It means I will fly to Germany and Austria to do research. I had wanted to see some of the places that figured in my narrative. But I am not jubilant. I am apprehensive. I phone a travel agent to learn about arrival and departure times. I don't sleep well. I phone a historian in Bremen, a cousin in Hamburg and my uncle Günther in Vienna to let them know about my visit. All are warm and welcoming on the phone. I feel a little better.

A few weeks later, at eleven at night Vancouver time, I call the archives for Sachsenhausen, a concentration camp that was located in Oranienburg, just north of Berlin. I am thinking about visiting the camp museum there.

When my mother told me that my grandfather had been taken to a concentration camp, she couldn't remember which one it was. "Maybe Dachau," she said. But I learned from reading the booklet about Kristallnacht that 163 Jews from Bremen had been sent to Sachsenhausen. So I wrote to the archives at both Dachau and Sachsenhausen to inquire about records concerning my grandfather. In due course, I learned that Dachau had nothing about him. Then a note arrived from Sachsenhausen, a couple of paragraphs typed under a stylized black and red crematorium. An archivist named Inge Ross wrote that "Willy Frensdorff born on 04.03.1881 had received the prisoner number 10452 in the Sachsenhausen concentration camp and was released on December 4, 1938."

I feel cold as I dial the long series of numbers needed to make an international connection. I have been intending to make this call for several days and am nervous about it. Last night I had troubled dreams in which I was on an alien planet, walking through corridors. At first the only life I saw was plant life, seaweedlike stuff undulating along the walls. Then suddenly, near my feet, I was transfixed by a single eye embedded in yellow and green scaly skin. I realized that the eye belonged to a reptilian creature, the shape of a large sea turtle but without a shell. The creature had many pointed teeth in a wide mouth. It growled and snapped. It bit me, but the bite was not terribly painful.

"Sachsenhausen," a woman's voice answers. I ask to speak to Frau Inge Ross. The woman goes to get her. While I am waiting, tinkly music plays — electronic bells. I do not recognize the tune. When Frau Ross comes on the line she says in response to my questions, "We are always open to the public. If you want to use the archives, just let us know when you are coming."

I hang up. I tell Gordon, "It's okay for me to visit." But in some ways I wish it weren't.

By Saturday, March 27, I am flying somewhere over northern Canada drinking tomato juice. I pick up a book but I scarcely know what I am reading. Instead, I am thinking about a line from one of my father's poems. "Reality is the strangest dream," he wrote in 1927. So it seems to me, too, suspended high above the earth, wondering what awaits me below. My first stop will be Bremen. I am hoping that if I am actually there I will be able to discover how Franz Stapelfeldt helped my grandfather to leave Sachsenhausen.

I land at the airport on Sunday. As I walk into the reception area, a man wearing a tweed jacket and high boots greets me. He hands me a red carnation. "Welcome to Bremen," he says. This is Dr. Peter Kuckuk. He is a historian with whom I have corresponded, an expert on the German shipping industry. He has invited me to spend my first night in Germany at his house.

We drive into the centre of the city and stop for coffee in the Schnoorviertel, a district famous for its tiny houses and narrow streets. Fishermen once lived here, but now the shops and restaurants cater to tourists.

I have sent Dr. Kuckuk copies of a few pages of my grandfather's diary, and he remembers that Willy Frensdorff mentioned building a new house in 1937. He wonders if I know where it was. "Weyerbergstrasse 3," I say quickly. He suggests that we drive past it on our way to his place.

And so, within a couple of hours of arriving in the city where my mother grew up, I find myself in front of a white stucco house with a steeply pitched roof. A white Mercedes is parked in the driveway. A low stone urn in the small front garden is filled with yellow pansies. I open the gate, cross the short walk and mount six steps to the front door. The landing is narrow. I think back to the night of November 10, 1938, when two uniformed men followed my grandfather up these steps. If all three of them had stood on the landing, they would have been very close to one another. The door is brown wood with a yellow glass panel in the middle. The glass is opaque and I can see nothing through it. I ring the doorbell. No answer. I ring again, but no one comes. I decide to look into the back yard. Fruit trees are still there, leafless now, and tall. I wonder if they are the same ones that my grandparents planted. I see the balcony where the scarlet runner beans climbed so high in the summer of 1939. I realize that, for some reason, I had imagined them growing up on the front of the house. I see no one.

We drive away and into the country past windmills and brown fields to an old red brick farmhouse. Dr. Kuckuk shows me to my room, upstairs in the loft. On its walls are posters of steamships and shelves laden with books and papers. We drink tea downstairs in the kitchen and talk about the Ag. Weser. I want to know whether the *Iller*, which returned to the shipyard from its test run on the evening of November 10, 1938, left that morning or the previous one. Dr. Kuckuk doesn't know of any records of its departure time, but he surmises, "It was a relatively small ship. I think one day would have done it." If that is so, then my grandfather would have left for work on the morning of the tenth. He would have seen the shattered glass, the painted slogans. When he changed streetcars at the Brill exchange, he might have smelled smoke. At two in the morning, members of the SA had set the nearby synagogue alight with gasoline-soaked rags.

I sleep fitfully and wake early. It is a windy day. Dr. Kuckuk offers to take me to the Ag. Weser grounds. Although the shipyard closed in 1983, some of the buildings are still there. Shipping companies now use the area as a warehouse for containers. On the way, Dr. Kuckuk tells me that Franz Stapelfeldt had been involved in a number of financial scandals. The ownership of his house on the Parkallee was always passing between him and the Ag. Weser. "Sometimes it was impossible to know who owned it."

At the gatehouse, a watchman speaks to us in *Plattdeutsch*, Low German, a dialect I cannot understand. Dr. Kuckuk asks him if we may have a look around. He explains that my grandfather worked for the Ag. Weser many years ago. The guard waves us through. We walk past a street sign that says, "*Use Akschen*." Dr. Kuckuk tells me that this too is Plattdeutsch and was how the local workers referred to the Aktiengesellschaft Weser. An *Aktiengesellschaft* is a company owned by several shareholders. *Use Akschen* means "our company." We see a large stone building with a massive front door and an elaborately carved portal. "Maybe your grandfather worked in here. This was an administration building," Dr. Kuckuk says. It is locked and no one appears to be inside. As we walk on towards the Weser River, I see large crates stamped with the names Hapag Lloyd and Lloyd Triestino. Dr. Kuckuk points to a line of leafless trees on the opposite bank. "In the pictures you see of ships being launched, those trees are often in the background."

I think about some of the ships my grandfather helped to build: *Athos II*, *Bremen*, *Gneisenau*, *Scharnhorst* and that last one, the small freighter, the *Iller*. I must be standing approximately where they were put into the water.

In the U.B.C. library, there is a picture taken in December 1934 when the *Scharnhorst* was launched. It's in a book called *Bremen in der NS-Zeit* (Bremen in the Nazi Time) by Herbert Schwarzwälder. It doesn't show the line of trees across the river from the shipyard or the ship itself; it's a photograph of all the dignitaries on the reviewing stand. Stapelfeldt is there and Hitler, too, the only occasion on which he visited Bremen. Wearing a trench coat and looking rather sour, the Führer stands on the right of Hjalmar Schacht, the minister in charge of the economy. To Schacht's left is Stapelfeldt and, beside him, General Werner von Blomberg, the minister of defence. The book does not identify the other men in the picture.

Stapelfeldt wears a dark coat or jacket. Despite his large peaked cap, he is obviously the shortest man on the reviewing stand; General von Blomberg is easily a head taller. Like Hitler, Stapelfeldt looks to his right and down. Like him, too, he has a small moustache. He doesn't smile either, although he does not seem quite as grim as Hitler. Actually, no one on the reviewing stand is smiling; they look like hard, determined men. And there is nothing in the photograph to indicate that Stapelfeldt is any different. A Nazi, you would say, glancing at the short man in the too-big hat. More than that — a Nazi in the core of the military-industrial complex. At the centre of power, with Hitler and von Blomberg and Schacht. One of them.

As I talk to Dr. Kuckuk on that overcast spring morning, I realize that he is not convinced that Stapelfeldt was unlike those other men. "He was clever," he says. "He may have supported both sides." I mention reading in Marssolek and Ott's *Bremen Im Dritten Reich* that when there were plans in the 1980s for a street to be named after Stapelfeldt, many people protested. Dr. Kuckuk nods. I remember too that the authors commented on how strenuously Stapelfeldt worked to obtain orders for torpedo boats, destroyers and submarines. Initially, at least, he was not opposed to the Nazi policies of rearmament.

As we walk back from the river, we hear a lot of noise

coming out of one of the buildings. We look inside and see that a dump truck is unloading broken bricks. Dr. Kuckuk shakes his head and says, "Garbage."

"My grandfather would not have approved!" I say. I know that he would have been unhappy to see a place once so productive now being used as a dump. Dr. Kuckuk tells me that Hans Koschnick, the mayor of Bremen, wept when the shipyard shut down.

Driving towards the city centre again, we pass through Bremen's industrial heart, factories and warehouses. Dr. Kuckuk points out the window and says, "This was all flattened after the war. Sixty per cent of Bremen was rubble." He pauses and adds, "I remember the bomb shelters. I still get anxious in a small enclosed room. I have to sit near the door. I can still see the walls dripping with water. It was so close. The sanitary conditions were awful. My mother had my sister in a pram. She had such a struggle bringing her into the shelter. Once, I remember, I lost my mother during a raid."

"You must have been so frightened."

"I was not afraid of the bombs," he says, "but of my mother's fear. I still have difficulty allowing myself to feel fear. I suppress it."

Our destination is the Staatsarchiv. It is housed in a modern glass-fronted building near the old moat. Once inside, we pass through a large, well-lighted room furnished with long narrow tables. People are working, poring over books and papers. Dorothea Breitenfeldt, whom I have come to see, has an office separated from this room by a glass wall. Dr. Kuckuk walks in without knocking. Later, I see that no one else knocks either.

We talk about my book and the progress of my research. Then Frau Breitenfeldt asks me if I would like to see Franz

Stapelfeldt's denazification files. I did not expect to be able to do so. "Of course I would," I say. A few minutes later, a young man hands me a cardboard box filled with papers.

About a year ago, Dr. Kuckuk had sent me a forty-seven-page typed memoir written by Franz Stapelfeldt. So I am familiar with much of his story. I know that he joined the Nazi party in 1937 and that he was honoured with the title *Wehrwirtschaftsführer* (War Economy Leader) in 1940. When the Americans arrived in 1945, they interned Stapelfeldt for nine months in Westerminde, and the German Communist party denounced him as a war criminal. But I also know that the Gestapo had arrested him in 1944 because of his involvement with a Berlin group opposed to Hitler and that he had been imprisoned until shortly before the war ended. I know that in 1946, when Franz Stapelfeldt's case came before a German court, an advertisement in the *Weser Kurier* invited people to write or speak on his behalf. Over two hundred people did, and among the documents in front of me now are their letters.

The opposition group that Stapelfeldt supported included people like Dr. Hans Gisevius, General Hans Oster and Admiral Wilhelm Canaris. When two members of the group, a navy officer and an army officer, landed in Dachau, Stapelfeldt offered to get them out. He had known the camp commandant, Piorkowski, before he joined the SS, because the man had sold office supplies to the shipyard. In September or October of 1941, Stapelfeldt went to Dachau, hoping to be able to free the two military men as well as four inmates from Bremen.

Here is Emil Theil, an Ag. Weser worker, recalling Stapelfeldt's visit. "It was a very joyful reunion. Piorkowsky [sic] withdrew for a few minutes and Stapelfeldt had the opportunity to speak to us. He asked about conditions in the camp, which we described to him briefly, and he promised to do everything for our release. He left 100 marks for each of the Bremer prisoners....I learned later from my daughter Hanna that my release cost Herr Stapelfeldt 20,000 marks, paid with an Opel 'Admiral' [a car] and the balance in cash. My daughter herself saw the receipt for this sum....Later, after my release, I thanked Herr Stapelfeldt, but he said that thanks were not necessary, he was after all in the gravy and this was a small thing."

Udo Meinecke, another shipyard employee, remembered that same meeting at the gate in Dachau. "Herr Stapelfeldt declared, 'Gentlemen, I will set you free.'"

I read letter after letter. H. Bruns, a watchman whose duty was usually at the main gate of the shipyard, writes, "Because we wore uniforms, we had to greet with the German greeting [Heil Hitler]. When I opened the gate for Herr Stapelfeldt and greeted him with a raised hand, he always answered, 'Good morning.'"

And here also is Friedrich Gefken: "Finally the big day came: it was March 1, 1941, when the Gestapo arrested me at the shipyard for high treason. I will never forget this day, not because it was the most dangerous for me, no, it was the best, because all my superiors, all the masters and foremen, Engineer Bertram, Shipyard Captain Hauptmann, absolutely all those who had something to do with the dockyard trade, came together to negotiate on my behalf with the Gestapo official, Ellmers....I can thank them for my head, because they contributed much to the fact that Stapelfeldt took on my case the way he did. Because I had openly described the whole Nazi Regime as a criminal state, the verdict was certain....He did everything imaginable to save my head....Paid my weekly wages, my holiday pay, my Christmas and potato money, and the cost of the proceedings (I myself did not have a red cent)."

I make careful notes about the letters I wish to photocopy. I still don't know what Stapelfeldt did for my grandfather in 1938. But now I can visualize him at the gates of Dachau. "Gentlemen," says the short plump man with the dark hair and the small moustache, "I will set you free."

I wonder if he had also paid someone to have my grandfather released. I close the cardboard box, my head full of questions. I will return tomorrow. The jet lag is beginning to catch up with me.

Dr. Kuckuk walks me to my hotel. Late that afternoon, after a rest, I decide to look for the old Gestapo headquarters. In the lobby of the hotel, beside the elevator, I see a notice about the performance of the play *Macbeth* at a theatre on Gastfeldstrasse. I am reminded that on Kristallnacht there was a performance of *Macbeth* here, too – the opera.

I don't know whether the Gestapo building still exists, but the street where it was, Am Wall, is not far. On the way, in the window of an antique store, I spot a poster with the English words, "Face Your Fears." Intrigued, I take a closer look and realize that it is advertising bungee jumping, an activity that has never appealed to me. But the message seems quite appropriate for my own undertaking.

I approach the moat, which is still filled with water and home to ducks and swans. Am Wall is on the other side, curving around the old part of the city. Once there really was a wall here circling the city, but Napoleon demolished it during his sweep through northern Germany. I cross the moat, turn to the east and minutes later find myself in front of Number 199. A plaque identifies the building as the former Gestapo headquarters.

This is where Willy Frensdorff met Regierungsrat Schulz and where my mother was questioned about the pistol in her father's night table. I pace in front of the building like a cat, not daring at first to go in. Across the street is a grassy bank leading down to the moat. A dense bed of gentian blooms on the bank. The flowers are as intensely blue as a flame.

My mother remembered double doors and yes, they are there – two sets with a vestibule between them. Glass framed by dark wood. Beyond the vestibule with its black-and-white tiled floor are corridors leading off to the left and right. In front is the staircase that my mother recalled. It spirals upwards. It is not exactly what I had imagined. I had pictured a much wider staircase and altogether a grander building with wood panelling along the halls. Instead, the corridors are covered in a beige enamel paint and the vestibule walls are tiled in green. Here at the foot of the stairs is where my grandmother, Melly, waited while her daughter talked to the two men upstairs. It was October. I picture her in a dark coat, a neat hat and gloves. She was probably wearing earrings. I remember that she was self-conscious about the size of her ear lobes. She liked to wear large round earrings to hide them.

Dorothea Breitenfeldt has told me that the offices in this building are still being used by the Bremen police but I see no one. The doors along the corridors are all closed. One has a sign with a heart on it and the words, "*Herz für Kinder*" (A heart for children). I knock on this door and then on another. No one answers. They're out, I think with some relief. I slip out into the sunshine.

Why am I so nervous? I am filled with an irrational, superstitious dread. I feel that to come back is tempting fate, a foolish hubris. I shouldn't be stirring things up. But at the same time, I can't seem to leave them alone.

St.-Petri-
Dom,
Bremen

21

Street Scenes

The following day, I visit Isarstrasse 26. The house where my
mother lived until she was twelve is covered in scaffolding. I
am trying to decide which angle would be best for a photograph when a tall, thin man, probably in his seventies,
approaches. With a smile, he asks me if I am a spy.

I tell him that I am interested in the house because my
mother used to live in it a long time ago.

"What was her name?" he asks.

"It was over sixty years ago. You wouldn't know her."

"But what was her name?" he insists.

Finally I tell him that she was Lore Frensdorff.

"Lore! Of course I remember Lore. They had a boat,
didn't they?"

The man introduces himself – Herr Mai. "It's too bad

about the scaffolding, we've had to do some repairs." He gestures up at the attic where my mother's bedroom used to be. "The top was burned during the war. It had to be replaced, but everything else is original."

He invites me in to meet his wife. She's a plump, comfortable-looking woman who also remembers my mother. Her aunt and uncle lived in the downstairs apartment while the Frensdorffs rented the second storey and the attic. "I often visited to be with my cousins," she tells me. "They were killed during the war – at the Front. That's why I inherited the house."

I sit in a chair in a bay window overlooking the garden. My mother used to run through this apartment, red braids flying, when she wanted to get into the backyard. She probably played with Frau Mai's cousins too.

The Mais want to know what happened to everybody. I tell them how my mother and grandfather escaped to Shanghai, how the family later emigrated to Canada, how my grandmother joined us in Vancouver and how she lived to be very old, ninety-one. Frau Mai keeps interjecting, as I talk, "Oh, it makes me so happy to hear that, so happy." I know that it really does, and my eyes fill with tears.

The next morning I walk to Obernstrasse. I stop beside the Karstadt department store. Did it happen here, I wonder? I consult my map. The letters and reports that Dorothea Breitenfeldt sent me about a year ago specified the location of the incident pretty exactly. I know that it occurred at a streetcar stop on Obernstrasse where you could catch the westbound Number 3. According to my map, there is only one such stop. This has to be it. I take a picture of the sign with its two Hs for *Haltestelle* (stop) and its large number 3. An elderly lady watching me assumes that I want a photo of the St.-Petri-Dom, a 1300-year-old cathedral whose twin spires are clearly visible from here. "Try again when the streetcar has gone," she says. "You'll get a much better view." When the car pulls away, she looks at me expectantly. In order not to disappoint her, I snap another picture.

Across the street, I see a bookstore called Storm Books and a discount clothing shop. A rack of cheap T-shirts takes up some of the sidewalk. Beside the clothing store is the stock exchange. To judge by the age of the building, it was there then too. The Karstadt store has large picture windows on the first floor and tall narrow ones set between thin ribs of light-coloured concrete on the upper floors — a modern façade. But the store was here fifty-six years ago on the same stretch of street.

Philipp Bechtloff must have been standing somewhere near where I am standing now. I don't know what brought him to Obernstrasse on the morning of Monday, February 15, 1937. He didn't catch the Number 3. He wasn't going to work. By then he'd lost his job as an engineer at the Ag. Weser. When he ran into Herr Gregor, another engineer on his way to the shipyard, he immediately started complaining. He said it was all the fault of Herr Stapelfeldt, Herr Frens-dorff, Herr Kalweit, Herr Behrens and Fräulein Luer that he had been fired. He told Herr Gregor that he was going to denounce them in *Der Stürmer* and *Schwarzen Korps*. He would see to it that they lost their positions. "Why don't you buy a revolver and shoot the Jew dead?" Herr Gregor snapped. When the Number 3 pulled in, Herr Gregor hopped on. "I don't need to buy a revolver, because I can do the thing legally," Herr Bechtloff yelled after him.

It is so quiet this morning that I find myself paying attention to the sound of footsteps on the worn cobblestones, a soft shuffling noise. I have the feeling that if anyone shouted, people would turn and stare with disapproval. But in

1937, cars weren't banned in the old part of Bremen, as they are now. It wouldn't have been so quiet. And perhaps a raised voice would not have been so conspicuous.

Later Bechtloff wrote a letter to Gregor. "I refer to our accidental meeting on Obernstrasse, where you said to me, 'Why don't you buy a revolver and shoot the Jew dead?' After that, you rode away on the Number 3 to the Ag. Weser. You probably felt it was urgent to report our conversation to the Jew, Frensdorff, immediately....You requested that I visit you at the Ag. Weser, which I did after a while....At this time your changed manner was especially noticeable....You suddenly tried to protect Frensdorff."

Now it is probably impossible to determine what lay behind Gregor's remark on that February morning. Was he exasperated with Bechtloff and being sarcastic? Or did Gregor actually mean what he said but think better of it for some reason by the time Bechtloff visited him? I don't know the answers. I'm inclined to think that Gregor didn't really want Bechtloff to shoot my grandfather, but I shiver a little, thinking of his ugly question on this cool day.

Bechtloff began grumbling about my grandfather shortly after joining the Ag. Weser. First, he complained to Richard Christiansen, who was the company's shipbuilding director and its liaison to the Gestapo. Then he wrote letters to Rudolf Hess, Hitler's deputy, and to Carl Röver, the district governor. He even threatened to shoot Willy Frensdorff.

At this point, Franz Stapelfeldt stepped in. According to a report that Christiansen later wrote for the Gestapo, Stapelfeldt asked to see Bechtloff. The report does not describe what happened at this meeting. But from it, I know that a few days later Stapelfeldt told Richard Christiansen that Bechtloff had violated company regulations concerning security. He was fired at the end of January 1937.

I walk up and down a little, reluctant to leave, almost as if I expect this particular stretch of cobbled street to yield a special meaning for me. I look in the windows of the department store. Today they are displaying a selection of children's clothing in neon colours, pink and green.

I remember from my reading that in August 1937 a hearing was held to see whether Bechtloff had been unjustly dismissed. Christiansen and Bechtloff were there as well as Bernhard Blanke, the head of the Nazi party in Bremen. Bechtloff said he believed his letters to Hess and to Röver had caused the trouble. After all, Stapelfeldt had reproached him about them. "You complained about us to the party!" he reported Stapelfeldt as saying.

After a lengthy discussion, Richard Christiansen proposed turning the matter over to the Gestapo for further investigation. He then wrote the detailed two-page report about the hearing that I read. In it, he commented, "Bechtloff is a self-confessed *judenfresser* [literally, a Jew-devourer] and has apparently set himself the goal of achieving order in Germany in this regard."

I start walking away from the streetcar stop in the direction of the cathedral, thinking about one last document I have concerning these events. It is a letter from the Gauleitung (the governor's office) addressed to Stapelfeldt. The letter writer did not type his name, only his title, Kreisamtsleiter. There is no signature on the document since it is a photocopy of the carbon he kept in his files.

Apparently Bechtloff had reported on a conversation with Stapelfeldt. He claimed Stapelfeldt had said, "You know that Frensdorff is a Jew. You complained about him to the party and you want to deprive him of his bread. You know that these days a Jew won't get a position any more and you know that Frensdorff is a patriot." The Kreisamtsleiter wanted to know whether Stapelfeldt had really called Frensdorff a patriot.

I remember being startled by Stapelfeldt's blunt language. He didn't try to disguise his intentions or his sympathies. He wasn't diplomatic at all. How did he get away with it? Did a Gestapo investigation ever take place? How did Stapelfeldt reply to the Kreisamtsleiter? What occurred as a result of Bechtloff's letter to Hess? I don't know. But at least I have some idea of how far my grandfather's boss went to protect him. When Stapelfeldt saw that he couldn't restrain Bechtloff, he got rid of him. I find myself agreeing with Bechtloff at least on one point. I think it was primarily the letters that cost him his job and not a breach of security regulations.

Reaching the St.-Petri-Dom, I notice a mediaeval stone lion holding a child-sized man between its paws and grinning. I snap a photo and wonder what happened to Bechtloff. What did he do during the war? Who suffered from his anger and fanaticism? It is not something I want to dwell upon. I see some graffitti scrawled on the stone wall behind the lion. It says, "*Gegen Rassismus*" (Against racism). Flower stalls huddle around the base of the church. I stroll through the colourful profusion – daffodils, tulips, azaleas, cherry blossoms. The great church bells begin ringing so loudly that the sound vibrates not just in my ears but through my whole body.

A couple of hours later, I am sitting in Café No. 103 not far from Obernstrasse talking with a red-haired historian, Dr. Inge Marssolek. We sit by the window. She orders cappuccino and I drink a local speciality – East Freesian tea, served strong and with chunks of crystallized sugar. Dr. Marssolek was one of the authors of *Bremen im Dritten Reich*, and now I am hoping she can help me to understand some of the events I have been researching.

When the Nazi party officials were considering Philipp Boohtloff's grievances in August 1937, he told them over and over again that he couldn't understand why Willy Frensdorff was able to continue at the shipyard. Bernhard Blanke had replied that authorities in Berlin were in agreement with Frensdorff's employment at the shipyard. Blanke stressed that they had known about the situation for a long time.

I want to know who those authorities were. "Was it Hess? The Ministry of Defence?" I ask Dr. Marssolek.

She sips her cappuccino reflectively. "You know, perhaps no one in Berlin knew about it. Perhaps the men just said this in an effort to keep Bechtloff quiet."

"And Stapelfeldt? Where do you suppose I might find something about how he got my grandfather out of the concentration camp?"

She shrugs.

"I suppose it's quite likely that nothing was ever written down," I venture. "Perhaps he just phoned someone."

"He probably did it informally. He knew all the right people. He got on well with Carl Röver. They used to get roaring drunk together. People would say that after one of these sessions Stapelfeldt always had new orders for the ship-yard and a number of people were released from concentration camp.

"Once Stapelfeldt had an employee who was half Jewish. He just struck out the word 'Jew' from the papers in the man's dossier."

We talk a little longer and then Dr. Marssolek must go. But before she leaves, she tells me that a friend of hers who hosts a radio program about history might be interested in my story. Two days later, I am drinking Pepsi in a sound studio at Radio Bremen. Peter Dahl, a dark, serious-looking man, is interviewing me for "Art und Weise" (Ways and

Means). I talk about Willy Frensdorff and how Franz Stapelfeldt, the general director at the Ag. Weser, helped him in 1937. I explain that I am trying to find out how Stapelfeldt managed to get my grandfather out of Sachsenhausen in 1938. When I am finished, Peter Dahl tells his listeners that anyone who has a suggestion about where I might look for this information should call the station.

The following morning, I am walking past the cathedral for one last look. I leave for Hamburg in the afternoon. "Hello, Frau Cornwall," I hear behind me. I am startled. Who knows me in Bremen? I turn around and see a man on a bicycle – Peter Dahl. "Three people phoned already," he says.

"I'm amazed," I reply.

"We were surprised too. We'll send a letter to you in Canada about their ideas."

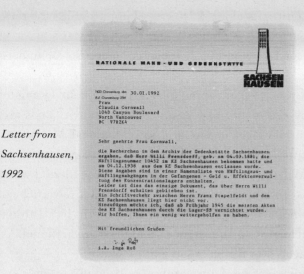

Letter from Sachsenhausen, 1992

22

I Won't Run Away

I leave Bremen, travelling by train across the sparsely wooded countryside of what was East Germany from Hamburg to Berlin. A boy of about eight and his grandmother are in my compartment. He is eating candies in the shape of bats and watching the fields for birds and animals. He's good at spotting them. His list grows longer and longer. "Four deer, two rabbits, one pheasant, one stork."

I too watch the flat land slip past the window. I read a little. And I worry. Will I get off at the right station? (Berlin has several.) Will I find my hotel? Will they have my reservation? Will I get lost going to Oranienburg? I make a list of worries. Writing them down makes them seem silly. Am I distracting myself this way? Am I trying to avoid something?

The next morning, I linger over breakfast. Three cups of

coffee. Then I walk along Kurfürstendamm towards the railway station. I have to go down four flights of stairs to catch the train for Oranienburg. I don't like going so far underground.

The ˙ ᵤp takes about three quarters of an hour. Oranienburg is the end of the line, a small brick station. Taxis are parked outside. I get in one and say, "National Mahn und Gedenkstätte" (National Memorial). I don't say, "Sachsenhausen." Will the driver ask me why I am going there? I wonder. He says nothing, turns his car into a narrow cobbled street. On both sides are trees, bare now, but in leaf I think their branches would almost meet, making a green tunnel. As the car travels over the stones, it rattles loudly.

Ten minutes later, I am standing in front of an iron gate. A sign says, "*Eintritt frei*" (Free admission). Still I hesitate. A woman in a kiosk says, "You can go right in."

"Where are the archives?" I ask. She explains how to find them. I turn left and walk around the former roll-call grounds where the SS used to assemble the inmates every day in order to count them. Thousands of men wearing striped uniforms were forced to stand in rigid columns here, sometimes for hours. Today there are only a few visitors, strolling slowly in groups of two and three on the flat grassy field.

I know that when Willy Frensdorff arrived in the concentration camp, he was wearing his second-best winter coat. But I don't know what time he walked through the gate. One hundred and sixty-three Jews from Bremen who had been incarcerated in the Bremen-Obslebhausen Prison on the night of November 10 were sent to Oranienburg on a heavily guarded train the next day. Dorothea Breitenfeldt has a list of who was detained in the Bremen-Obslebhausen Prison that night, and my grandfather's name is not on it, though the armed men seized him on November 10, in the evening.

Perhaps the car that picked him up from his house on the Weyerbergstrasse brought him directly into the camp. Perhaps it took him to another detention centre in Bremen. He may have joined the group of Bremen Jews at the railway station in the morning. Then he would have been with them on the forced march from the Oranienburg train station to Sachsenhausen. I can't say which is true.

I scoop fragments out of the past, but much slips through the net. I know it was cold that November. Did Willy shiver when his head was shaved and when he had to exchange his wool clothes for a prisoner's uniform?

Now it drizzles. Sometimes for a moment the clouds part and a little blue sky is visible. Then the wet flagstones gleam in the watery sunshine. I walk slowly along the perimeter of the camp. I reach a white door. I push it open and go in. A group of five or six people are seated at a table, evidently having a meeting. A slight blonde woman gets up. She says, "You must be Frau Cornwall." I nod. "Frau Inge Ross?" We shake hands.

"Perhaps this is not a good time. I'll come back in an hour."

"If you don't mind."

I wander. I notice the colour of the cell-blocks – some dark green, some grey, all trimmed in white. The paint is peeling. I go into what was the infirmary with its white tiled floors and walls. I see the counters that the doctors used when they experimented on people. They too are covered in white tile, and they have drain holes. Outside I see the leafless trees beyond the walls. I think that they would have been leafless while my grandfather was here too. I hear the birds sing. I take a picture of the words "*Arbeit Macht Frei*" formed out of iron bars, part of a gate. I notice other people taking the same picture. I visit a cell-block that was occupied by prisoners who were being punished especially severely. I peer through iron bars at bare rooms containing narrow cots. Straw sacks served as mattresses. Plaques tell visitors the inmates' names and something of their stories.

I visit a small museum. On one wall is a map giving the location of the concentration camps in Germany. The points are dense. They even include ships moored off the coast. I didn't know about the ships, nor about the many small camps with unfamiliar names.

I see a notice board on which people have posted letters. "Would anyone having information regarding the whereabouts of…" I look at a display showing a prisoner's uniform and wooden shoes. I take a few notes. Between 1936 and 1945, almost 100,000 people were put to death here. Communists, trade unionists and liberals were the first prisoners.

In November 1938, 6000 Jews were brought to Sachsenhausen, and between 1938 and 1942, 1417 Jews were killed. In the beginning, the corpses, with numbers painted on their chests, were sent for cremation to Berlin in wooden crates. The SS called them "meat boxes." Later a crematorium was built at the camp. Its foundations can still be seen. A sign asks visitors not to step on them.

As I walk back to the archives, I hear a woman say to a man – in German – "One should see a place like this once in one's life." I see another woman twirling a red umbrella. The gesture seems out of place. Why is she doing that? I wonder. I notice a couple arriving with a bouquet of red roses. They seem uncertain about where to put them.

Frau Ross seats me at a small desk in a well-lighted room. I face metal shelves holding boxes of files. She brings over the one that contains the document I have asked to see. It is the only record she has on which my grandfather's name appears. I examine it carefully.

When camp officials stripped inmates of their money and personal effects they issued receipts. If the prisoners were lucky enough to be released, their property was returned. These transactions were the business of the "Money and Effects Administration." The department prepared lists of who had arrived and who was leaving. The document I am reading is one of these lists — "Jews Released on December 4, 1938." One hundred and eighty-three Jewish men were set free that Sunday. My grandfather was the thirty-eighth. The typed list of men's names, birth dates and prisoner numbers is signed by an Obersturmführer. I cannot read his signature. I ask Inge Ross if she can make it out. She looks at it and shakes her head. "I don't know who he was. We never concerned ourselves about those people."

According to another document Frau Ross gives me, there were 12,226 men in the camp on December 4. They fell into eight categories. The largest group, Jews, Politicals and Antisocials, numbered 5036. Malingerers and Gypsies totalled 4850. Those in "Protective Custody" (some of whom were Jews) were tallied at 1722. In the latter group, one was listed as "absent on leave."

"Were people let out for short periods?" I ask, thinking that perhaps I have misunderstood. "I have never heard of such a thing."

"Neither had we, until we started to look at the documents."

As I hand back the papers, I remember a story my mother told me. "My grandfather had to shovel dirt and stones here. First he would move a pile to a certain spot. Then he had to shift it back and start all over again. Do you know anything about that?"

"The prisoners had to do a lot of unnecessary work," says Frau Ross. Then she shows me a book, *Mein Leben im Kz*

Sachsenhausen (My Life in the Sachsenhausen Concentration Camp) by Harry Naujoks. "It covers the period that your grandfather was here. You can buy it in our bookstore on your way out."

I had hoped to discover something about how Stapelfeldt helped my grandfather to get out. On that score, the documents are mute. The SS destroyed many of the camp records in the spring of 1945. Perhaps they shredded the letter I would so much like to have seen.

I phone for a taxi to take me back to the train station, and the dispatcher says, "It will be about ten minutes. Don't run away!"

I say, "I won't run away," and then think how odd it is that I should be uttering that sentence in this place. While I wait, it begins to hail. I button up my coat and search for a place out of the wind.

The train I catch for Berlin is marked "Wannsee." I think immediately of the Wannsee Conference held in January of 1942. In a villa by a lake, Reinhard Heydrich led a meeting about Europe's Jews. There government and Nazi party representatives settled the details of the "final solution." The policy meant death for millions, including, of course, my grandparents Rudolf and Regine Wiener.

The train reminds me of their story. Learning about Regine's death started my investigations. But it has always been harder for me to think about Regine and Rudolf Wiener than about Willy Frensdorff. This is probably because he escaped and they were trapped; his story had a hero and theirs did not. Will my visit to Vienna make it easier to write about them?

Rudolf and Regine Wiener, Vienna, March 1939

23

City of Dreams

An arrow of longing
An arrow of love,
Flies to a faraway and unhappy destination.
Flies and still does not come to rest
In the dark chaotic life
Far from the homeland
Far from peace.

My father wrote these lines in Shanghai on August 2, 1947. The unhappy destination that the arrow did not reach was Vienna. Although the war had been over for two years and his Austrian citizenship restored, he had no plans to return. From his office on the fifth floor of the *North China Daily News* building, he watched the sampans on the Whangpoo River.

Sometimes he thought about another river. He would think about it later, too, long after leaving Shanghai. And his feelings for the city where he grew up would become a piece of my childhood.

A Sunday morning in Vancouver. After the breakfast dishes were cleared away, my mother laid a checked cloth over the kitchen table. She dusted it with flour and then she began to roll out a lump of dough, a simple pliable mixture of flour and water. First she used a rolling pin but then, to make the dough even thinner, she slipped her hands underneath. She stretched it with the backs of her hands and pulled at it, using the balls of her thumbs, not her fingers. She knew just how far she could go; she didn't tear it. When the dough was done, it was transparent. You could read a newspaper placed underneath.

There are other kinds of pastry, made with yeast, that people call strudel. But I still think of this as the authentic one. This is the one with the dance, the difficult balance. The closer you come to the ideal, the higher the risk of failure.

Beside me was a bowl of apples I had helped to peel and slice. They were sprinkled with sugar and cinnamon, almonds and raisins. My mother didn't mind if I tasted a few. I liked to feel the grainy texture of the sugar against the moist surface of the apple.

After my mother eased the sheet of dough back onto the cloth, she brushed it with melted butter and covered it with a layer of toasted bread crumbs. They would absorb the juice of the cooking apples. If there were not enough breadcrumbs, the excess liquid would create a hole in the delicate dough and the strudel would fall apart. But if there were too many, the result would be dry and bland.

My mother tipped out the bowl of apples onto the prepared dough and dropped a few teaspoonfuls of jam onto the mound. Using the checked cloth, she rolled up the pastry, pinched the ends together and brushed the outside of the strudel with more melted butter.

After it was baked, it had to cool a little. Then I got to dust it with confectioner's sugar. I liked this job. As the spoon scraped against the metal sieve, I watched the tiny white points of sugar snow down. When I was finished, I moistened a finger to pick up the sugar that had fallen on the plate beside the pastry.

In the afternoon my father made espresso coffee and whipped cream. We had blue-and-white dishes. We sat at a round table, the same one my mother had worked on to make the strudel, now wiped clean of flour. The sun streamed into the kitchen. Our forks lifted the strudel, aromatic, slightly warm and draped in cream. I savoured the contrast between the crunchy buttery pastry and the soft apples, which had almost lost their original shape and melded into one another.

My father put Viennese music on the record player, popular songs mostly. Richard Tauber's "Songs of Old Vienna" was a favourite, the vinyl well worn. A faint crackle weaving around Tauber's sweet tenor voice seemed to belong to the occasion as much as the melodies did, and the sound of the violins.

When I arrive at the Franz Josef Bahnhof in Vienna on April 7, 1993, there is no music. It is early; the railway station is quiet. I say good-bye to an East German woman and her daughter, with whom I shared the compartment since Berlin. "I can hardly believe I'm here," she says. I nod. It seems strange to me, too, but for different reasons. She is caught up in the excitement of being in a place that East Germans were not allowed to visit for a long time and I in being somewhere that has occupied such a significant part of my imagination.

When I was a child, listening to my father's records did not make me sad. But by the time I was twenty it did, though I did not know yet that my father had fled Vienna, that his parents had been deported from that city. I remember one Christmas when I came home to visit my parents for two weeks. I was twenty-two and I had been teaching English in Germany. Near the end of the holiday, I stood in my parents' kitchen, my head on Gordon's shoulder, weeping.

"Why are you crying?" my mother asked me.

"It's the music," I said.

She wasn't convinced. "It's because you're going away again and Gordon's staying here."

"I think it's the music," I repeated.

"Mommy, why do you listen to it if it makes you sad?" Thomas once asked me years later. I was playing the songs in my living room on an afternoon when he was home from school with a cold. I didn't know how to answer him.

"I don't understand the songs," he said. "Why do they make you sad? Are they about people dying? Sometimes I cry when I hear, 'She's leaving home.' That's about it."

I gave him a hug and he started singing another Beatles song. "Hey Jude, don't make it bad, / Take a sad song and make it better."

Thomas's question made me think about the content of those old Viennese songs, something I had never really done before. I realized that they are not often about dying. Mostly they are concerned with love: "Down in Lobau I kissed a girl, / Her eyes as blue as the violets in the meadow"; springtime: "In the Prater the trees are blossoming again, / in Sievering the vineyards are turning green"; and, of course, Vienna.

If I had to leave this beautiful place,
Then my yearning would have no end,

Then from far away I would hear a tune
That rings and sings,
That draws and attracts me.
Vienna, Vienna, only you
Will always be the city of my dreams.

Rudolf Sieczynski's "Vienna, My City of Dreams" is wreathed in nostalgia, but not just because it is old. It was nostalgic even when it was first written. The copyright on it is 1914. Did Sieczynski somehow already sense the troubles, the diaspora that would come? Did I, listening to the song so many years later, somehow sense the ache of it too?

In the deserted railway station near the Danube Canal, I find a phone booth and call my uncle. He lives in Perchtoldsdorf, a village on the city's outskirts. I tell him that I will get there by a combination of U Bahn and S Bahn and then reach his house by taxi. Outside the station, the roads are slick. It has been raining, though now a weak sun shines. I keep seeing elderly men who look like my father. Like him, they are short, have curly white hair, pale blue eyes. Like him they wear green Tyrolean hats. Around me is his voice. Years of speaking English have softened but not eliminated his accent.

In German, the word for a Viennese is *"Wiener"* – my father's name. And mine too, until I married. In a way, that makes these people family. And yet not family. This was the place my father had to flee. Still, the fear that I was so acutely aware of in Berlin has receded. And in a way this is strange. I was so afraid of Sachsenhausen. But Willy Frensdorff was only there a little over two weeks. And he was rescued. Someone cared enough about him to get him out, despite the risk. Here my grandparents had no one to rescue them. But in Vienna I feel at home. How can anything bad happen at home?

There is a long wait for the S Bahn. It takes me about two hours before I come to Perchtoldsdorf. And then the taxi has difficulty finding my uncle's house in the hills above the village. I have been here twice before, once when I was twenty-two and spending a year teaching in Munich and once when I was twenty-four, with Gordon, but I had forgotten that my uncle lives so far from the centre of town. I had forgotten the vineyards all around, their gnarled branches sear and brown still. Despite the April sunshine, it is cold, and the vines are dormant.

When I finally arrive, my uncle is waiting on the street, watching for me.

"We had started to worry," he remarks.

My Aunt Anna is on the steps. She smiles. "I said you didn't have to make yourself anxious about Claudia."

I remember the house better — the large garden, the French doors leading to it from the living room. The sofas and the television are still in the same place. My uncle gives me the same bed I had on my earlier visits, in an alcove off the living room.

"Have you had anything to eat?" he asks.

"Not much," I answer truthfully.

He makes me an espresso with the same kind of Italian machine that my parents have and gives me a couple of buns with butter.

My Uncle Günther is taller than my father, thinner, eight years younger. He doesn't stoop the way my father does. His white hair is straight. His eyes are hazel. He wears glasses. "Your father and I don't look at all alike," he says. "I used to ask my mother if she was sure there wasn't a mixup in the hospital."

"You have the same hands, though," I tell him. They are square with blunt fingers. His feet are like my father's, too.

Small, narrow, neat. Not like mine, which are big for my height and wide.

My uncle returned to Vienna in April 1949 with Anna, who was his second wife. After the war, Vienna, like Berlin, was divided into Russian, British and American zones. The city was poor and good jobs were hard to find. My uncle struggled for several years before becoming a salesman for a pharmaceutical company. He bought his house when Perchtoldsdorf was still part of the Russian zone. "Some people worried about living here, but I didn't think the Russians would bother us," my uncle says. His daughter, Susi, still lives in Vienna; his son, David, has moved to Stuttgart.

Sitting at the dining room table, I sip my coffee slowly, savouring its excellent flavour. My uncle and I chat idly, getting reacquainted. I compliment him on his English. He says, "I learned it in Shanghai. But your father already spoke it when we arrived. You know that application I made for Russian citizenship, the one that interested you so much..."

I nod.

"Your father helped me with that. You should ask him if he remembers."

"I don't think he does. He was so surprised to hear about it," I reply, now wondering why my father didn't fill out an application for himself at the time. "But I'll ask him when I get home."

The next day, I go to the Austrian National Library in the centre of Vienna. The building that houses it is called the New Hofburg. Constructed between 1881 and 1914, it was the final residence of the Habsburg dynasty. I walk across the Heldenplatz past a statue of Prince Eugen, a famous general. Then I go through a handsome wrought-iron gate and across marble floors to a librarian. I tell her that I would like to look at newspapers in the reading room. She asks me to fill out a form. I struggle with the German. Where it says "Signature," I naturally sign my name, and then the librarian tells me that what is wanted is the number of the material I am requesting. I fill out the form again and walk down a curving staircase to the reading room. Behind a counter is a young man wearing jeans. He smiles at me but shakes his head after looking at my form. It is still not correct. I want to see newspapers of different years. Each year must go on a separate line. I try again. This time he is satisfied. But he tells me it will take a couple of hours before the newspapers can be brought to me. I go for a walk.

I stroll into the Burggarten behind the library. I come upon a statue of Mozart surrounded by playful, naked cherubs. His name is written in gold leaf, and on the lawn in front of the statue yellow pansies are planted in the shape of a treble clef. Immediately behind is a tree, its leaves still tiny. Points of bright green form a halo around Mozart's white marble head.

Two hours later, I am back in the reading room. Piled high on the desk in front of me are leather-bound copies of the *Wiener Nachrichten*. I start with March 15, 1938: "The Führer's greeting to German Vienna."

German troops had streamed across the border on March 12. On the fourteenth, Hitler arrived in Vienna. It was a warm spring day, the blue sky cloudless. The gardens were showing their first pale green.

Wearing a brown uniform, riding in an open grey Mercedes, Hitler came in a long cavalcade down Mariahilferstrasse to the inner city. With a start, I realize that I took the same route myself this morning, on streetcar Number 58 from the Kennedy Bridge.

On that March afternoon, people lined the streets, waving flags and singing folksongs. There were swastikas everywhere. As the Mercedes drove by, people shouted and raised their right hands in the Hitler salute. At the Heldenplatz, just outside the front door of the building I am now in, there was a reviewing stand. The Parliament Buildings nearby displayed a giant picture of Hitler framed in evergreens interwoven with flowers. There were drums and martial music. Hundreds of thousands of people thronged the centre of Vienna. The paper quotes a sausage seller who said he had never done such a brisk trade.

From Heldenplatz, the parade made its way along Opernring to the Kärnter Ring and the Hotel Imperial, where Hitler spent the night. On the way, he passed the Burggarten. I wonder if the memorial to Mozart was there then. Was it too draped in a Nazi banner?

The reading room is quiet. Occasionally, I hear the rustle of paper or the scrape of a chair leg. I read on. October 1, 1938. The day my father and my uncle left Vienna. It was dull and overcast, cool, with occasional showers. Hitler and Chamberlain had just signed the agreement in Munich that ceded Czechoslovakia's Sudetenland to Germany. Chamberlain said, "I believe it is peace in our time." Headlines in the *Nachrichten* reported that in London and Paris champagne was sold out, so relieved were people that the threat of war had subsided. My father and my uncle saw their parents for the last time, and the German tanks rolled through the Bohemian forest between Helfenberg and Finsterau.

I move through 1939, 1940, 1942, and then decide to go for coffee. The Hotel Sacher is not far away, behind the Opera House on Philharmonikerstrasse. On the way there, I pass a line of brightly painted horse-drawn carriages called *Fiakers*. Business is slow today. The horses draped in their brown-checked blankets look sleepy.

In the coffee house, the headwaiter, dressed formally in a

black suit, white starched shirt and black bow tie, quickly finds me a place. Beside me, a woman is sitting with a young boy about my Thomas's age. For him, the woman orders Coca-Cola and Sacher torte. This is the chocolate cake that Édouard Sacher created for Prince Metternich and for which the hotel he founded became famous. I am amused when I notice that the boy eats only the icing on the cake. My children would probably do the same. I ask for coffee with *schlag* and apple strudel. When the strudel comes, I pay close attention to its taste. The baker has been too cautious. The pastry is not quite thin enough and there are too many bread crumbs. My mother's is better. But I am happy to sit in the old-fashioned room with its dark red walls, velvet upholstered chairs and small round tables. I drink my coffee slowly and watch the schlag gradually dwindle in the glass cup.

When I return to my uncle's house in the late afternoon, I find my Aunt Anna searching for an envelope containing recent photographs of her youngest grandson. Aunt Anna is eighty, a couple of years older than my uncle, and forgetful.

Beside the dining room table is a carved Chinese chest made of dark wood, one of several pieces she brought with her from Shanghai. She decides to look in one of the drawers and pulls out a jumble of photographs and papers.

My aunt shows me photographs of my cousins when they were children. My uncle finds an identification card he had to use until 1955 when the Russians finally left Perchtoldsdorf. And then he hands me an envelope. It is addressed to Mr. Günther Wiener at the General Post Office in Shanghai, China. "Via Siberia" is written underneath my uncle's name and underlined. In the lower left-hand corner is a stamp with a large red *R* on the left side and the words "Wien 2" in black. Stamped on the back, in black and red ink, are swastikas and eagles and the word "*Geöffnet*" (opened). The censors had looked inside. Above the stamps are written "Regine Sara Wiener" and an address, "Tuchlauben 16." This is my grandmother. When I first read her name I am puzzled by the unfamiliar "Sara." And then I remember. This was the name that she, like all other Jewish women, was forced to adopt.

"Take it," he says to me. "It's another letter from my mother."

"I'll make a copy and give it back."

"No, no. I don't need it. It's not very pleasant. She makes so many reproaches." I glance quickly inside the envelope. I see two sheets of paper written on both sides in blue ink. The date is May 24, 1941, about a year later than the last letter I have seen. But the handwriting is difficult. I will have to wait for my mother to help me read it before I know what it says.

"I wonder," continues my uncle, "what my brother thinks of all this. It was tragic. We couldn't bring them out. We had no money. The passage to Shanghai was so expensive."

"You know that my father never spoke of it."

"I think he is a bit ashamed of his Jewish background. I don't know why."

"Do you have any other letters?" I want to know.

My uncle shakes his head. I didn't expect him to have any at all. I feel lucky to get this much.

The following morning, I cross the Au Bridge, which spans the Danube Canal. Cherry trees, their blossoms still tightly shut, not showing any colour, line both banks of the canal.

I walk three blocks down Augartenstrasse until I come to Kraftgasse. It is a narrow street, a block long. On both sides are unremarkable apartment buildings. I am looking for 6/10. I find Number 6 with its carved wooden double doors and an unornamented concrete façade. A sign to the left of the door says that the building was reconstructed after the war. I take a picture of it and of another building on Augartenstrasse visible from the doorway of Number 6. It has a turret and a lion carved into a sixth-storey lintel. There is no Kraftgasse 10. Perhaps that part of the building was never rebuilt. But there is a bit of scrubby grass and a bench, Pensioners' Park, according to a small sign. Perhaps this is where Kraftgasse 10 used to be.

A few weeks before I left Canada, a Viennese Jewish organization, the Israelitische Kultusgemeinde, had responded to an inquiry of mine. They informed me that Kraftgasse 6/10 was my grandparents' last address in Vienna. This street is in the second district, the old Jewish quarter, into which Jews from all over Vienna and from other parts of Austria were crowded. After September 1941, they had to wear the yellow identifying star and couldn't leave the district without official permission. By November, their freedom of movement was restricted even further. All emigration was halted. I don't know the date on which my grandparents moved here, but I know the date they left the district. The Kultusgemeinde had told me that they were deported on May 6, 1942. I'd been happy to receive the information. And puzzled by my happiness. Why was it better to know exactly?

I am reminded now that after reading the letter I dreamed about visiting my grandmother on Kraftgasse. Gordon was with me, and I remember her saying, "*So ein hübscher Kerl*" (What a pretty fellow). Her remark pleased me, but I was rather surprised by her use of the word *hübsch*. Then the dream changed. I was watching a black-and-white film about the deportation of children. Long lines of them were waiting to be taken away. A bearded man wearing a red vest — the only colour in the dream — held one little boy by the hand and walked with him in the other direction. Who was the boy? My father? And who was the man in the red vest?

I look around me. My grandparents walked on this stretch of sidewalk. But I don't know whether they went to work, shopped for groceries or took their shoes to be repaired. I wonder if Kraftgasse 6/10 was one of the *sammellagern* (assembly camps) I had been reading about the night before in the April 1993 edition of a magazine called *David*. In an article entitled "Die Zentralstelle für Jüdische Auswanderung in Vien, 1938-1943" (The Central Office for Jewish Emigration in Vienna from 1938-1943), the author, Gabriele Anderl, explained that these assembly camps were established early in 1941. Before that, the Central Office had delivered summonses to the homes of those Jews selected for deportation. People were informed of their impending transport and told when to appear at a designated depot. However, warned about what was to happen, many Jews attempted to escape. Thus, the Central Office changed its technique. In February and March of 1941, selected Jews were ordered to move into sammellagern. There they were closely guarded. When they were finally told to ready themselves for their transport, they found it difficult to escape.

I recall that the *Wiener Nachrichten* for May 6, 1942, was full of war news. The Japanese had taken the island fortress of Corregidor in the Philippines. British destroyers had been damaged in the English Channel. And on the eastern front, some German soldiers who had been trapped behind Russian lines for three months managed to break out. There was not a word, however, about the thousand Jews who were leaving Vienna that day.

It was a thin paper, perhaps because of wartime shortages. Still, there were advertisements for movies. *The Great King* was playing in several movie houses; *Eve* was at the Ostmark VII and *Hotel Sacher* at the Schottenring Cinema. The State Opera House was showing *Salome*, and the City Opera House, *Rigoletto*. There was also an announcement that a new botanical garden, the Alpine Garden, was about to open. It would display not only well-known varieties of flowers such as alpine roses and gentian but also rarer ones. The Alpine Garden was located a few blocks east of the Aspang Railway Station. It was from there that Rudolf and Regine Wiener left Vienna.

They were brought to the station from Kraftgasse in a truck. Waiting for them was what was called a "special train." People were crammed in ten to a compartment. Only a jug of water and a few loaves of bread were provided for each car. When the cars were full, they were locked and the windows closed. Somewhere farther east, the people were transferred to open freight cars.

Gabriele Anderl writes that in 1942 over 25,000 people – a total of twenty-one transports – were sent to Minsk. Most became the victims of mass shootings; some died horribly in mobile gas chambers, on trucks.

Unlike Sachsenhausen, Kraftgasse 6 is not a place dedicated to memory. There are no memorial sculptures, no exhibits, not even a plaque. Ordinary life has reclaimed the street. In front of the apartment house across the road, a bicycle is parked. A woman wearing a brown jacket rings a doorbell and goes in. It is as if my grandparents had never existed.

I decide to visit the nearby Augarten, a huge formal eighteenth-century park, orderly and spacious. Inside the park is a palace painted in yellow and white, a lofty building with lovely tall doors and windows. I go inside. The palace houses a porcelain factory and a shop that sells the exquisite product. There are fine vases and delicate teacups decorated with flowers. I think my daughter, who likes pretty things, might enjoy one, but my heart is not in it. I walk out again and over the bridge that my grandparents were forbidden to cross.

Later that day, I go to Hietzing, Vienna's thirteenth district. It includes Schloss Schönbrunn and its large park filled with statues, fountains and long tree-lined alleys. Here too are three- and four-storey apartment buildings and large villas widely spaced. Gardens nestle behind walls.

Although the Number 60 streetcar would take me a distance down Hietzinger Hauptstrasse, I prefer to walk. It is Good Friday afternoon. Easter is a major festival here and the Monday a holiday, but today the shops are open. People on the street carry bags brimming with groceries. Bunches of flowers, daffodils usually, perch on top.

Number 108 is a turn-of-the-century building with a grey-and-white façade. This was where my father lived for more than twenty years, from the time he was ten until he left Vienna. The front door is painted in two shades of brown. I look through a small window in the door and see that in the foyer are black-and-white tiles, then a short flight of stairs leading to a hallway. I try the handle. It is locked. A sign beside the door announces that one of the tenants offers *energische Therapy Shiatsu* (vigorous shiatsu therapy). In the basement is a carpet store.

My uncle has told me that the Wieners had the ground-floor apartment on the right side of the building. The window closest to the door looked out from their kitchen. Now whoever lives there has a red geranium plant inside. It is tall and scraggly from having spent the winter reaching for the sun. When I try to imagine my grandparents waving good-bye from that window, the red geranium keeps getting in the way.

The second window from the door faced out from the bedroom that my uncle and my father shared. My uncle told me that when he was young, the street was cobbled and the carriages would rumble as they travelled over the stones. Standing here, I remember one of my father's old songs, "My pride is that I'm a true child of Vienna / I drive a fiaker."

For many people the fiakers are part of something vanished and beautiful. But for my uncle, the memory of carriages outside his window is not a happy one. "Sometimes the fiakers would go all night. My brother and I wouldn't be able to sleep because of the noise."

The fiakers would be on their way to villages on the outskirts of Vienna, where innkeepers would serve the potent, slightly sour wine that the Viennese hills have been producing since the third century A.D. The patrons would usually drink outside, seated at rough tables under the shelter of large trees. In the fall, the innkeepers would hang out cedar boughs as a sign that the new wine, known as *heurigen*, had arrived. It was especially prized, but the drinking went on all year. An old song goes, "I must go to Grinzing once again, / To the wine, to the wine, to the wine…"

"I think a whole generation of men were affected," my uncle has told me. "My father would go from one Heurigen to another, eating and drinking. Once I went with him. After a while, he sent me home with a piece of Sacher torte and schlag. He was gone for two days. It was awful. Sometimes he was so drunk, we would find him lying in the street."

My uncle remembers his father and an uncle filling their breast pockets with cigarettes and then distributing them on the street to whomever wanted them. Another time it was a barrel of sausages. There were flamboyant gestures, but not much money. "When I was thirteen, my mother pawned a watch I had so she could buy us some cocoa," my uncle said. "I remember that my mother's relatives thought she should get a divorce, but she didn't want to. She worried about what people would say."

Standing there in the street, I recall a story my father once told about himself as a young man. It was a summer night, his bedroom window open to let in the breeze. "I can't stand it any more!" he'd shouted and slammed the window shut. I'd understood that he was exasperated and upset. I knew that his father was too fond of his wine, that there were difficulties about money. But I thought he'd slammed the window to relieve his feelings as one might slam a door or throw a shoe. I hadn't understood why it was important to shut the window on a hot summer night. Now I did. He would shut out the noise. The fiakers.

The young Walter would create his own world. He would write poems in that room. But no one knew about them. His friend R— didn't. His brother Günther didn't. "I wrap my loneliness / Around me like a dark coat."

As I walk back along Hietzinger Hauptstrasse the cars seem to make almost no sound at all.

*Letter from Rudolf Wiener to his son Günther
in Shanghai, 1941*

24

The Last Letter

About a week after my return from Europe, when my mother and I read the letter that Uncle Günther gave me, there is a surprise. Although the handwriting is very like my grandmother's and the envelope was addressed by her, the letter itself was written by my grandfather, Rudolf Wiener. He signed it, "Your parents," but I can tell he had written it from what he said. "Now I've heard from all of them," I think.

I am sitting with my mother in her kitchen when we make the discovery. I have the tape recorder with me so that I can record her reading of the letter. Later, at home, I will translate it into English.

When my father walks into the room, I tell him that the letter I brought back with me was from his father, not his mother. He nods but does not stay to listen to my mother reading it, returning instead to the living room.

Rudolf Wiener wrote the letter from Tuchlauben 16, a couple of blocks from St. Stephen's Cathedral, the fourteenth-century church in the very heart of Vienna.

"Dear good Günther: We acknowledge your dear letter of April 20th which came on May 21. Today two packages arrived in good condition and you gave Mama great joy. We thank you heartily for your attentiveness....However, we haven't had any news from Walter since the end of November even though I asked him to write a card at least every month."

"I'm a little bit annoyed at this man," my mother interjects. "He was not a good daddy. How could he ask your father to write wonderful letters? I mean, I don't think I would have written a guy like that."

She turns back to the letter. "I cannot understand why he has become so indifferent," she reads, then stops again. " 'Has become?' " she asks. "Was he less indifferent before?"

I don't know whether my father was indifferent or not. I don't even like to think about the question. So I say nothing, and we continue with the letter. I find its normal tone remarkable. It reveals nothing of the extraordinary circumstances in which it was written. Was this because it had to pass through censors? Because Rudolf didn't want to worry Günther? Because he didn't allow himself to see or feel what was happening? Or was it a relief to forget about the situation for a little while?

In the spring of 1941, Günther was living in Shanghai but, as I gather from the letter, he was considering a move to Tientsin. Rudolf had some advice for his younger son. "Please discuss it carefully with Walter, because one can't count on promises from people that one has known only for a short time. Tell us about your final decision....As far as I have informed myself, Tientsin lies 700 km. north of Shanghai, a port with a very good climate. So in this regard one doesn't need to worry."

How had he been able to inform himself? I wonder. Was this before Jews were forbidden to use public libraries? Did he still own books, an atlas? Or did he ask someone? (Later, when I pull out my own atlas to check, I find that his information was quite correct.)

"Concerning the pictures which would have made us happy, as you can see from the censor's enclosed note, they were not with your letter. Perhaps you didn't enclose them, and we ask you to send them along next time."

Rudolf also mentioned some of the relations – Uncle Oskar, Uncle Viktor, Uncle Alfred. He gave an address in Prague. "Please write a card. They ask about you in every letter and it would make them very happy. Uncle Zitle is ill; he had to have an operation. Otherwise I don't know what to report about the relatives. I only get news every two or three months. Muni [his brother-in-law who had gone to England] has not yet written a line."

"It made me grin when I read your remark that the beer tastes good," my mother reads.

She glances up. "He has to think right away that somebody is going to drink lots," she says. "What is there to grin about if someone says that the beer tastes good?" She turns back to the pages in her hand.

"Because of my illness," Rudolf's letter went on, "I have to abstain almost completely, and you will be amazed that I now drink only a bottle a month with Mother. Unfortunately, I also had to give up my beloved pipe, and I miss them both....I suggest to you in this regard not to overindulge in the good even though I wish it for you with all my heart."

My mother stops reading yet again, clearly exasperated. "I think someone like this should never say that," she criticizes. "As if it is such a pleasure to have loads of it. I mean a little bit is a pleasure."

"Well, he knows...," I say, thinking that Rudolf understood very well the reasons for not drinking too much.

"Well, he knows," my mother agrees, "but Günther never had the inclination to – I've never seen that. So you can see, they didn't know each other.

"Funny – when I married your daddy, I didn't know about the concentration camps, but since I didn't have the best experiences with my daddy's relatives, I thought, now your daddy had no relatives in Shanghai – ah, easy."

My mother turns back to the letter. "Of former friends," Rudolf wrote, "I hardly come face to face with anyone because of the distances. We are both healthy and in spite of everything look good. Again, all the best. Heartfelt greetings from us. Write soon. Naturally the same heartfelt greetings to Walter. Stand by each other. Concerning financial matters, we are convinced of your good will; perhaps it will be possible later. Enclosed is a note from the censor's office. Your parents."

The censor's note, dated May 21, 1941, said, "The enclosure mentioned, several pictures, was missing as the letter was opened. Before complaining to the post office, would you ascertain from the sender of the letter whether this was actually sent along." The note explained that if the pictures had really gone astray in the mail, the person who sent them should inform the post office in the country where the letter was mailed. In any case, "compensation will not be provided for the loss of the material."

As I fold up the two sheets of paper, I am struck by the fact that although Rudolf may have perceived my father as indifferent, he did not appear to bear a grudge. "The same heartfelt greetings to Walter," he had written. I tuck the letter back into its envelope stamped with eagles and swastikas. And I find myself recalling something my mother had told me a year earlier. She and my father had been fast asleep in the bedroom on the west side of their house. It was quiet, the middle of the night, and there was very little traffic. The tops of the tall trees in their garden swayed noiselessly. Suddenly, in the darkness, my mother was awakened by blows. My sleeping father was hitting her. "Walter, you're having a nightmare!" she exclaimed as she shook his shoulder.

Slowly he opened his eyes. "I was dreaming that I met my father."

When I first heard this story, I was surprised that my father still harboured such bitterness towards Rudolf. I was also startled by the way he expressed his feelings. I had never known him to hit anyone. He did not spank me as a child, and I can remember how critical he was of corporal punishment of any kind.

Reading this last letter does not help me to understand why my father is still so angry with Rudolf. But it does make me wish that he would forgive him. "Perhaps then he could forgive himself," I think. When it is time for me to leave, my father is dozing. I slip out of the house without speaking to him.

My uncle has told me that Rudolf Wiener was the eldest son of a family of seven − five boys and two girls. After Rudolf came Viktor, Richard, Arthur, Ottla, Jetty and Oskar. Rudolf's father, Adalbert, had remarried after his first wife died, and Oskar was the son of the second marriage. Rudolf met my grandmother, then Regine Moldau, in Vienna. My father was born in 1906 at their home on Blumauergasse in the second district. My uncle was born eight years after my father. By then the family had moved out of the Jewish quarter to 175 Mariahilferstrasse. The Wieners lived there until my father was about ten, when they moved to Hietzing.

"It wasn't a happy marriage," my father said to me once. He told me about a long fiaker ride from Perchtoldsdorf during which his mother and father quarrelled. His father said over and over again, "*Das arme Mädchen, das arme Mädchen*" (the poor girl). My father did not know what girl Rudolf was speaking about or what the matter was with her. But he was distressed to hear the argument.

According to my father, Rudolf wanted to study after finishing school. He liked to write. But his stepmother complained that there wasn't enough money for such an impractical course of action. Instead, Rudolf was sent from his home village of Chleby to find work in Vienna.

I have fragments of stories, but I don't know how to put them together. I cast around. I become curious about the village of Chleby. It was near Nymburk, in what is now the Czech Republic. My father has fond memories of the place and of his grandfather, whom he visited several times as a little boy. The young Walter travelled to Chleby all by himself on the train from Vienna, and a man called Konopec picked him up at the station with a buggy.

I visit a local library to see whether there might be a map detailed enough to show the village. The librarian isn't able to find one, but a young man overhears me talking to her. Speaking slightly accented English, he introduces himself and tells me that his father, who still lives in the Czech Republic, is very knowledgeable about local history and geography. He offers to write to his father to see whether he might know anything about Chleby.

A couple of weeks later, the young man, Jaro Bares, comes to see me, bringing a translation of his father's letter, which is written in Czech. The father, whose name is also Jaro Bares, has visited the village twice on my behalf. Mr. Bares, Sr., reports that my great-grandfather's house, Number 60, still stands in the middle of this agricultural community of a couple of hundred residents. But it is empty, and no one takes care of it.

From an old book that Mr. Bares refers to as the Village Chronicle, he learned that in 1892, my great-grandfather donated money to the local fire brigade, and in 1900, he helped to establish a farmer's reading circle. He also discovered that all of my great uncles, with the exception of Rudolf, fought for the Emperor in World War I. One of them, Arthur, died in a prisoner of war camp in Russia.

After Mr. Bares had returned from his second visit to Chleby, the mayor phoned him to say that a woman named Mrs. Havlasova, who worked for Adalbert Wiener from 1914 until 1918, when he died, was still alive. The mayor had been to see her. Now in her nineties, she remembered how once a week the old gentleman would lead members of the local Jewish community in prayers at a small chapel.

Later Mr. Bares sends me a picture of my great-grandfather's house. I see a beige stone building with a red tiled roof, shuttered windows and a door. An overgrown grassy track leads to a metal gate. The yard beyond is thick with weeds; bushes are wild, unpruned.

I show the photograph to my father. He points to one of the windows. "That's where the living room was. And beyond the house was a river."

"Isn't it incredible that it's still standing?" I say.

My father nods but says nothing, and I am left wondering what he thinks. I don't know whether it pleases him to see this place where he once was happy or whether it makes him sad.

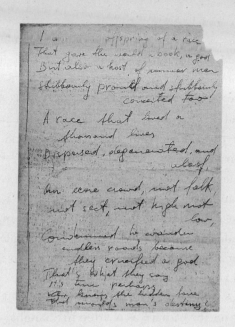

25

Poem by
Walter
Wiener,
Shanghai,
1947

Hidden Forces

It is the middle of August, 1993. I am sitting with my family in my parents' living room. The occasion is Karl Frensdorff's visit to Vancouver. He is the distant relation from Delaware who sent me a copy of the Frensdorff family tree, and with whom I have corresponded ever since. When a nephew's wedding brought him to the West Coast, he decided to visit us as well.

This evening he is explaining his theory of how the Frensdorffs got their name. He tells us that Frensdorf is a small village near Bamberg in southern Germany. "I've been there. It's a tiny place. I don't think a Jewish family would have settled there. They probably lived in Bamberg. But at the time that Jewish families were required to take German surnames, they took the name of this neighbouring village, because there were already so many Bambergs and Bambergers."

He believes that the reason the family's name is spelled differently from the village's is due to a nineteenth-century German spelling reform. An effort was made to eliminate unnecessary letters. Up until that time, *dorf* (village) had been spelled with two *f*s. The village dropped its second *f* because of the reform, but the family saw no reason to change their name.

My father mentions that, in Austria, Jews were ordered to take German names during the reign of Maria Theresa. He tells us that sometimes the officials who were in charge of the matter decided on the names and gave people silly ones like *Kochlöffel* (cooking spoon). And then he says, "I would like to read you a poem."

He asks my mother to bring him the booklet of his poems. The one he wants was written in Shanghai in 1947, in English.

> *I am an offspring of a race,*
> *That gave the world a book, a god,*
> *But also a host of minor men*
> *Stubbornly proud, conceited too,*
> *A race that lived a thousand lives,*
> *Dispersed, bigoted, and aloof,*
> *An eerie crowd, not folk, not sect,*
> *Condemned to wander endless roads*
> *Because it crucified a god.*
> *That's what they say, perhaps it's true.*
> *Who knows the hidden force that moulds man's destiny?*

Karl nods appreciatively. "It's good."

"Would you like to hear another?" my father asks.

"The shrimps are ready," says my mother. "Why don't you read it after dinner? Is that all right?"

216

"It's not all right," my father mutters. But he closes the booklet and we come to the large round table where we always sit. We have prawns cooked in garlic, sourdough bread and several salads. After eating dessert, an orange cake covered with chocolate icing, my father is tired and goes to bed.

The following Thursday, Karl Frensdorff and my parents visit me for lunch. It is a hot day, and I have set a table in the garden. We are drinking wine and eating smoked salmon sandwiches when suddenly my father's plastic chair tips over. No one sees how it happens.

We right him almost immediately, but his back hurts. He and my mother go home early. His pain gets worse; a few days later, he is admitted to the University Hospital. He moans whenever he has to move and sleeps for hours. Sometimes he refuses to eat or take his medicine. His confusion increases. When I bring him some pictures my children have drawn and pin them on a cork board beside his bed, he says, "I wonder whether the Japanese authorities will approve."

The doctors are puzzled by his condition. Has the accident accelerated the inevitable deterioration that Parkinson's disease causes? No one seems to know. I feel he is slipping away from us. When I visit, we don't talk much. I hold his hand and play Viennese waltzes for him on my children's tape recorder. Will he recover? Will he come home again?

And strangely enough, just when my father is so ill, I learn how my grandparents, Regine and Rudolf Wiener, died. I find the information in the U.B.C. library, but through a circuitous route. Were it not for the Archiv des Österreiches Widerstandes (the Archive of Austrian Resistance) in Vienna, I would not have located it. I had heard from the Kultusgemeinde in Vienna that this archive might be able to tell me something about my grandparents' last years in Vienna. I had hoped to visit the archive while I was in Europe, but it was closed for the Easter holidays. So I wrote when I returned home. A couple of months later, I received a letter from Dr. Elizabeth Klamper, who recommended *Jüdische Schicksale* (Jewish Fates), a book her archive had recently issued. I ordered a copy.

The volume, seven hundred pages long, arrives in late August. It consists of interviews with Viennese survivors of the Holocaust as well as some background material written by historians to help readers understand these first-hand accounts.

I read the densely printed text slowly. When I come to the section dealing with the deportations, I discover that the transport carrying my grandparents, the one leaving for Minsk on May 6, 1942, arrived at its destination five days later, on May 11. From a footnote, I learn that this information was included in a report written by an SS man, Unterscharführer Arlt. I learn also that his account has been reprinted in *Unsere Ehre Heisst Treue* (Our Honour Is True), one of a series of books about the Third Reich published by Europa Verlag.

On a Saturday in September, I drive out to U.B.C. I plan to visit my father, who is still in the hospital there, and to look for *Unsere Ehre Heisst Treue* in the stacks. I go to the library first, and on the ground floor I find the book I want – a large, red, leather-bound volume. I walk over to the hospital reading it, barely aware of my surroundings.

I see that it consists of reproductions of war diaries and reports written by members of the Waffen-SS who were ordered to follow the German combat troops into the Soviet Union. The documents in the book were written between June 1941 and January 1943. Sometimes they are scarcely legible, and sometimes they contain typing errors or penned-in corrections.

The layout and the style of the reports vary considerably.

Sturmbannführer Magill gave the number of people his
group killed between July 27 and August 11, 1941: "The total
sum of plunderers and others shot: 6526." But he was obviously a well-educated man who also made observations about
the area's culture and economy. "The living conditions are
everywhere similar, poor wooden houses with straw roofs....
It is noticeable that during the Polish time very fine schools
had been built." Other men confined themselves to descriptions of troop movements and lists of the Russian and Jewish
dead.

Unterscharführer Arlt commanded a group of ten men,
the second platoon in the First Battalion of the Waffen-SS
stationed near Minsk. His reports went to Hauptsturmführer
Störtz, who was in charge of the First Battalion.

On May 4, 1942, Arlt and his men began to supervise the
digging of pits at a place that he described as "the property of
Kdr." They were finished four days later. "On May 11," he
wrote, "a transport with Jews (1000 head) from Vienna
arrived in Minsk and was taken immediately from the railway station to the pit. The platoon was positioned right next
to the pit for this purpose." ·

That was it, then, the place where Rudolf and Regine
had died. The event that had so disturbed me when I first
learned about it five years ago occurred on a Monday in May,
within walking distance of the railway station in Minsk.
Strange to know this. And strange also to know who had
given the order to shoot. I had never intended to find out who
killed my grandparents. Although I often described my
research as detective work, I considered this to be a metaphor.
I had not expected the statement to contain so much literal
truth.

"Knowing more of the details makes it better," I think as
I walk past some brilliantly red vine maple trees. But why?

I've asked myself this before without coming to a conclusion. Because there is a person I can hold responsible? Somehow I don't think that's it. I don't feel better because I can blame someone. "Being able to fix the time and place puts the event on a more human scale," I say to myself. But what does that mean? Does that make it more bearable? How? It is not less tragic for being more precisely known.

I pause outside the hospital for a few minutes before going in. I see that *Unsere Ehre Heisst Treue* reprints four of Arlt's reports, dated between May and September of 1942. He was very cool about what he was doing. He expressed no emotions, though in June he did request permission to take his yearly leave when circumstances allowed it. "My last leave," he reminded Störtz, "was in August 1941. Unterscharführer Lipps says he will stand in for me."

"The transports of Jews arrived in Minsk at regular intervals and were entrusted to us," Arlt recounted. "On June 27, we began an action at Baranowitsche....In the course of this action, we emptied the Jewish ghetto, Slonim. On this day, approximately 4000 Jews were put into the earth....

"From 25.7 until 27.7 new pits were dug. On 28.7 a major action in the Russian ghetto in Minsk. 6000 Jews were brought to the grave. On 29.7, around 3000 German Jews were brought to the grave. The following days were occupied with the cleaning of weapons and tidying up....The conduct of the men on and off duty is good and gives no reason for complaint."

"No reason for complaint," I repeat to myself as I push the elevator button for the floor of my father's ward. How could Arlt write that?

When I get to my father's room, he is sleeping peacefully. My mother is also there. I show her the book and explain what I have learned from it. "Don't tell Daddy," she says. He otire a little and I take his hand. He looks at me and falls asleep again. I think that perhaps I will tell him when he is more alert.

On the way home, I think about Arlt. Who was he? Where did he come from? Did he survive the war? And if he did, was he punished after? Did he ever marry? Have children? Grandchildren? If he had grandchildren, are there some my age? Do they know? Or is this the Arlt family secret? I decide to send a letter to the Simon Wiesenthal Documentation Centre in Vienna to see whether someone there might be able to answer my questions. Weeks pass. I receive no reply and I wonder if Rudolf and Regine's story has come to a natural conclusion.

I continue to think about Willy Frensdorff, however. Radio Bremen sends me the addresses of three institutions and a person to whom I might appeal for more information about Franz Stapelfeldt. By this time I have already tried archives in Hanover, Hamburg, Koblenz, Berlin, Bremerhaven, Jerusalem, New York and California, to no avail. I eagerly follow the radio station's suggestions, but they too yield nothing.

I am beginning to feel I have reached the end of the road when I finally hit upon a productive lead — in my parents' black trunk. It surprises me to learn that I still have not plumbed its contents. The clues come out of a brown envelope on which my grandmother, Melly, had written "*Wiedergutmachung*" (restitution) with a red pencil. I have been aware of this envelope for some time but have not paid it much attention. My mother has told me that my grandmother appealed for compensation because Willy had been taken to a concentration camp. Although he had died by the time Melly started legal proceedings, she had thought that as his widow she might be entitled to something. "But she didn't get anything," my mother said. I took my mother's word for it; the brown envelope was not important.

When I finally decide to read the documents inside, I discover that my grandmother had, in fact, received about 16,000 marks in compensation for the special taxes that Willy paid when he left Germany and for the expenses of his trip. I also find several reports written by officials with the Bremen Office for Restitution. On August 23, 1960, someone called Lüken recounts that Willy Frensdorff was brought to the concentration camp in Oranienburg and that he was freed after much effort. I already know this, of course, but what interests me are the other documents to which the report refers: statements from people like Erwin Schulz, the former head of the Gestapo in Bremen, and Franz Kruppenbacher, a colleague and friend of my grandfather's. These letters supported my grandmother's application, but they are not contained in the brown envelope. I write to the archives in Bremen to see whether they have copies.

One frosty November morning, a fat envelope from Bremen arrives in my mailbox. I think the weight of it is a good sign: Dorothea Breitenfeldt must have found something. Inside there are a number of documents, including some of the papers I had asked to see.

My grandmother, Melly Frensdorff, first wrote to Erwin Schulz in June 1954. This was just six months after Schulz had been released from Landsberg Prison, to which he had been sent after a trial in Nuremberg. (He had originally been sentenced to twenty years but had launched an appeal for clemency in 1952.) My grandmother's letter began, "Dear Oberregierungsrat." The regime that made this man an important official was gone. Yet to my grandmother, he still was not plain Herr Schulz. Melly wondered whether Schulz could confirm the following statement: "In the year 1938, after the well-known Jewish pogrom, my daughter and I came to you in person about the release from Oranienburg of my husband, Oberingenieur Willy Frensdorff, then employed at the Ag. Weser. I had a letter of recommendation from General Director Stapelfeldt. My husband was then released on your order during December 1938."

When I ask my mother whether she recalls this meeting with Schulz, she says, "No." She thinks for a minute and then shakes her head. "Strange, I can't remember anything about it."

But Schulz remembered. On the back of my grandmother's letter, he wrote, "Although I am not able to recall the exact dates, still I can declare under oath that the facts of the case described on the other side are correct. I know about the case because I was then chief of police in Bremen."

W. Parchman, another former Gestapo man whose name appears in my grandfather's diary, also signed a statement. Although he didn't mention a letter of recommendation from Stapelfeldt, he acknowledged that Willy Frensdorff was imprisoned after the pogrom in 1938 and that the order for his release had come from Schulz.

I still don't know what Stapelfeldt wrote in his letter, but one of my questions about these events has now been answered: Schulz was the man to whom he appealed. The documents settle an issue that has perplexed me for some time. But they create a complication, too.

Included in the packet from Bremen is a statement that my grandmother, Melly, made to the Office for Restitution on June 3, 1960. She said, "I remember that after Oberregierungsrat Schulz ordered the release of my husband on December 5, 1938, my daughter and I waited every day for the return of my husband. I think it was five days later, that is, on the tenth, that I told the above-mentioned Schulz that my husband had not returned home. I was informed by the above-mentioned gentleman that he had intervened on my husband's behalf and I must have patience. When on the following days neither my husband nor news of him arrived, I went again to Herr Oberregierungsrat Schulz. But this time I wasn't allowed to see him. If I reflect, I would say that my husband returned on December 18 at the earliest. It could have been a couple of days later. In any case, he came back a few days before Christmas. I know this so exactly because we were still under the impression of his return on Christmas Eve."

The documents from Sachsenhausen showed that Willy Frensdorff was freed on December 4, 1938. Was my grandmother mistaken, then? Or were the camp records wrong? I don't suppose I will ever know. But if my grandfather really came home on the eighteenth, this raises further questions.

I know from reading *Invisible Walls* by Ingeborg Hecht that on December 12 an order was issued for all Jewish detainees over the age of fifty to be released. Was my grandfather still in prison on the twelfth? If so, was he freed because of this order? Would he have been able to leave Sachsenhausen even without the intervention of Stapelfeldt and Schulz?

The new documents do not shed light on these questions. But they do provide more details, add texture to my picture of the events. From Franz Kruppenbacher's letter to the Office of Restitution, I learn that the test run of the *Iller* took place in the North Sea, and that the ship left from Bremerhaven, a port on the east bank of the Weser. My grandfather had not been brought home in the company car, as my mother thought. He used his own car and parked it in Bremerhaven for the day.

Reading this, I wonder whether on the morning of

November 10 he drove straight north from his house to the docks in Bremerhaven, bypassing the shipyard. Perhaps he wasn't in the centre of Bremen before work; perhaps he didn't see the signs and the broken glass or smell the smoke from the ruined synagogue that morning. Perhaps he didn't know what was in the wind until midnight when the two men accosted him on the front steps of his house.

Kruppenbacher remembered that although my grandfather drove back to Bremen, some of his colleagues returned by train. In the station in Bremerhaven, they heard my grandfather's name being broadcast over the loudspeaker. Willy Frensdorff was ordered to report immediately to the police.

"Through the efforts of General Director Stapelfeldt," Kruppenbacher recalled, "Willy Frensdorff was returned to his family a few days before Christmas. I visited Herr Frensdorff at home. He told me quite openly that he and the other unfortunates in Oranienburg were treated much worse than animals."

In her book Hecht writes about her own father, who also had been released from Sachsenhausen in December 1938. Like Willy Frensdorff, he had been arrested during the Kristallnacht pogrom. "It had been intimated to my father and all the others released that day in December 1938 that anyone who spoke of his detention outside would be in serious trouble." When my grandfather was freed, he apparently did not worry about getting into trouble for speaking about his imprisonment. But my parents did — for more than fifty years.

Claudia Wiener, Easter 1956

Voices

In 1991, after I was well into my research, my father told me about something that had happened in Vienna. "I was stopped on the street and asked, 'Are you a Jew?' Then someone else said, 'But he doesn't look Jewish!'"

"What did you say?" I wanted to know.

"I can't recall."

"How did you escape?"

"I don't remember. Perhaps it happened to a friend of mine. Perhaps a friend told me."

At the time, I recorded this conversation in my notes, describing it as "a scrap of a story." There was so much I didn't know. Which street? What year? How had it ended? Nevertheless, I kept returning to the incident, thinking that it might reveal something to me if only I knew how to look at it. "The two lines somehow condense the horror," I wrote in my diary. "The street confrontation. 'Are you a Jew?' The question — the one asked so many times. The reply: 'But he doesn't look it.'"

At first my father had said that he was the person being questioned, and then he became unsure of this. Why? Was he the man in the story, but the memory so painful that he couldn't bear to think so? "Perhaps it happened to a friend." Was this his way of putting distance between himself and the event? Or *had* it, in fact, happened to a friend and so aroused his sympathies that it was as if it had happened to him? Or was his confusion the result of old age? Was I wrong to treat forgetting like an action, like something for which reasons could be found?

"Are you a Jew?" The question that so disturbed my father came up again and again in my diary, in conversations and in correspondence. One Saturday morning in November, I phone my mother to tell her about a subtitle that my publisher is considering for my book — "A daughter uncovers her family's Jewish past."

"But my father wasn't Jewish," my mother protests. "He'd left all that. Your father too. You're throwing them back in the water again, after they tried so hard to escape it, to put it behind them." My mother speaks quickly, hardly pausing for breath. I am surprised by the strength of her feelings.

I say, "But even if your father wasn't Jewish, *his* father was. And Daddy's parents were. I wouldn't have started all this if they hadn't been."

"I know, but..." Now she stops to recollect. "Sometimes my father would say, 'Here they come with the whole *mishpokhe* — the relatives.' He didn't get along with his family. Helmut was charming, but he never had a good job. Clara's first marriage ended in divorce and her second was unhappy.

My father didn't like that, and he didn't approve of Arthur, either. He was fond of his mother, though; he was always very kind to her."

Our conversation drifts to other subjects. I can hear my children fighting in the next room and then Talia comes to me wanting comfort. My mother and I hang up.

I feel as if I have come back to that snowy afternoon when my mother and I sat in my car talking about what she had learned in 1933. "Being Jewish is a matter of religion," she had said. "It is something you choose. It was Hitler who made it a matter of race – something you cannot choose." It was her view, and was probably her father's as well, that once Willy converted he was no longer Jewish.

So did I have just two Jewish grandparents? And what about my father? Did he cease to be Jewish that day in September 1938 when an Anglican minister in Vienna baptized him? And what about me?

I think back to a couple of other conversations. One was with a friend, Bronia Sonnenschein. She is herself a concentration camp survivor, and I met her through the Vancouver Holocaust Centre Society. One afternoon we were having tea in her apartment, a cheerful place full of flowers and china figurines and pictures of her grandchildren. She talked to me about living in the Lodz ghetto and about being shunted from camp to camp. She told me about being part of a death march to Theresienstadt and how she had been liberated by a single Russian soldier on horseback. "You are free. You can go home now," he had informed the prisoners.

Our discussion moved on to the subject of my book. "I think you would have been what we call a righteous gentile," Bronia said. I didn't reply, but I was surprised by her remark. "I'm not exactly a gentile!" I thought.

On another occasion, at a party where I was talking about

my family, a woman commented, "So you're Jewish. How interesting!" Again I said nothing. But I thought, "What do you mean, Jewish? Nobody in my family practises."

How confusing it all is. In my diary I write, "If this were a novel, I would probably convert to Judaism or do something dramatic — go on a long trip — have some major insight into my character. But I don't. I am beginning perhaps to understand the depth of my outsideness, that's all." Questions continue to roll through my mind, unresolved, and then someone from the Holocaust Society phones with a piece of news about my grandparents that I want to relay to my father.

It is December. He is now home from the hospital. He still can't walk; he spends most of his time in bed, using a wheelchair when he does move around the house. I sometimes talk to him about my book. He listens, but I am not sure how much he really absorbs.

I visit on a Saturday. My parents and I have lunch in the kitchen, sitting at their round table. I think about Regine: "Perhaps you could send me a little tea for Father." And about Rudolf: "The same heartfelt greetings to Walter." I reflect on the picture I have of Regine and Rudolf together and about the power they had to shape events so long after their death.

"You know, Daddy," I say, "this spring, the Vancouver Holocaust Society will be putting your parents' names on a memorial. Now that I know their birth and death dates, those dates can go beside their names. I had asked the society to do this a while ago, but I had to wait because new names are added only every couple of years." My mother smiles. My father looks at me. He says nothing. I don't know what he thinks.

As the weeks go by, my father grows more and more frail. A physiotherapist starts coming to the house to encourage him to walk. The nurses who have been helping to care for my father since he came home from the hospital try exercises. My mother engages a Chinese doctor who prescribes herbs and practises the art of Chi. By giving my father his Chi, Dr. Shen thinks that he may help him to walk. Dr. Shen is a recent immigrant to Canada from Shanghai. By coincidence, he studied medicine at St. John's University, where my father taught during the war. I think how strange it will be if Dr. Shen manages to rehabilitate my father. It will be as if once again he is rescued by the Shanghai connection. But though my father is less stiff and more comfortable after Dr. Shen's visits, he still doesn't walk. And it becomes increasingly difficult for him to breathe and to swallow.

One evening in the middle of January, my mother phones me. "I think this is the end," she says. My father is gasping for breath. I grab my coat and drive across town. When I get to my parents' house, my mother opens the door and says, "He's gone." I go into the bedroom, still wearing my coat. My father's face is pale, unnatural for him — his complexion was always so ruddy. The nurse's aide on duty stands by his bed. "Touch him," she suggests. I stroke his forehead. His body is still warm. My mother pulls up the blankets and tucks them around his shoulders.

The next day, my children come. They want to have one last look at their grandfather. When the undertakers roll a stretcher bearing his body down the long front walk, Thomas and Talia follow. They wave and call, "Bye-bye, Opa!" as the blue van pulls away. "His last journey," my mother says. I wipe my eyes.

In the days that follow, my mother and I write letters and receive sympathy notes. We prepare for a memorial service and a reception. I start the final revisions of my manuscript. After my mother reads the second draft, she phones me. "Perhaps we should have told you when you came of age, perhaps when you married Gordon. But we didn't think so much about it. I know that Daddy didn't want you to have trouble at school. He didn't want you to have to fight. That's why you were baptized." And then she adds, "I'm glad the bubble burst, and that Thomas and Talia know. But your daddy was never so sure. After Günther wrote to you, Daddy asked me, 'Will this be good for the children?'"

I had always thought that my father would like holding my book, feeling it in his hands, riffling through the pages of the bound volume. Now I wonder if it would have worried him to see it. Would his anxiety have outweighed his pleasure?

Towards the end of January, I dream that my father comes to my house for a visit. He is a ghost, but a very substantial one. Wearing khaki pants, suspenders and a white shirt, he looks the way he did the day of his accident. My family and I are sitting around our dining room table, having a meal. My father doesn't eat. But he sits and watches us. He tells us that if there had been a cure for Parkinson's, he would have stayed with us a little longer. He is a very comfortable sort of ghost, not the least bit frightening.

The next night, I dream again about my father. I go into his bedroom to see his body. His head moves a little and I wonder if he is really dead. "Are you sure?" I ask someone in the room. It could be my mother, or a nurse. "How strange that he died," I say to the other person in the room. "Only yesterday, he started to walk again." And then in my dream I remember him doing this. I recollect him sitting up and then reaching for the grips my mother had installed on a bookshelf beside the bed. Slowly, with my mother's help, he stands and then unsteadily begins to walk out of the bedroom. But this never happened: the memory is only dreamed.

When I wake, I recall the couple of occasions my mother and I had actually tried to help my father stand. He had reached for the grips beside the bed and then both of us, with our arms under his, had pulled him to his feet. But he had not been able to stand without our support or walk at all, even slowly. It is hard to get used to the idea that the hopes my mother and I had for my father are now without foundation. He will never walk again. There is nothing more to try. And my questions about the meaning of the past? He is not there to help me answer them.

I had always planned to end my book with a chapter entitled "Missing Identity." "The last chapter will be a chance to reflect upon the nature of cultural identity and assimilation," I wrote in a brief outline. "My parents did not want to burden me with conflicts centuries old. They had come to Canada to make a fresh start. Like many immigrants, they wanted to escape the past. What was lost? What was gained?"

Now, having come to the end of my investigations, I find these questions exceedingly difficult to answer. Perhaps they are the wrong questions. What would my life have been like if I had always been aware of my family's history? Would it have been better? Or harder? I don't know.

Towards the middle of March, I am having lunch with my mother. I ask her once again how she feels about the subtitle that my publisher proposed. "In the end something else might be used. Or it might be worded a little differently. But I think it should be considered," I say.

"How do you feel about it?" she asks me.

"I'm okay with it."

She shrugs her shoulders and smiles. "I guess I am too. After all, it's what happened, isn't it? It's in the book, anyway. What's the fuss about?" I feel that this is a significant moment, a turning point, although I am not sure of its consequences.

Easter weekend, 1994. We are staying with my mother-in-law, Charlotte, in a cabin she and a friend of hers own. It is on the shore of Sheridan Lake, about six hundred kilometres north of Vancouver. In the summer we get to the cottage by boat, but now the lake is frozen and this afternoon we crossed it on skis. I carried a pack on my back filled with clothing and Gordon pulled an aluminum toboggan to which we had lashed food boxes and a bag filled with stuffed animals.

After dinner, sitting beside the stone fireplace and savouring the warmth, I say, "Last year I was in Vienna on Good Friday. I remember how cold it was. Even though I wore a shirt, a sweater, a jacket and my cape on the street, I still shivered." I see myself walking along Hietzinger Hauptstrasse and Kraftgasse, two streets in the same city, but so very far apart.

I recall that an Australian friend, Felix Carrady, once asked me in a letter, "Do you now have to redefine yourself utterly?" "As for redefining myself," I wrote back, "a process has begun. I feel, however, that I am not in charge of it. The process I am engaged in is making me feel less and less defined."

Reflecting now about Felix's question, I realize why I answered the way I did. I have become aware of myself as part of a much larger entity – my family. I carry their voices wherever I go. In some ways, I feel less unified than I once did. But I also know that my sense of connection with my family has become far stronger. There is my son, Thomas: *You started the book because of me.* My uncle Günther: *The lady standing up was our mother, who died in concentration camp*; and my grandmother, Regine: *My longing to see you two is terrible.* I hear my father, Walter, at the age of twenty-one in Vienna: *And reality is to me the strangest dream*; and my daughter, over sixty years later on another continent: *Dreams have lots and lots of gravity.* Then there is my grandmother, Melly, walking at night in the mountains while the German tanks were driving towards Moscow: *Yesterday evening was such beautiful moonlight... and I went a short way up to the edge of the forest. Then nearby I heard the call of a rutting stag. Oh, that sounds frightening!* I listen to my mother, Lore, at nineteen: *My dear Daddy, I think everything is weeping for you because since we've been back in Germany it has been raining almost constantly*; and her father, Willy, in Shanghai, a month before he died: *I have finally made myself free.*

The voices follow me, even here, to the Cariboo. Even here I cannot separate myself from what I have learned about my family and what happened to them over fifty years ago.

The transport identified as "Da 210" left the Aspang railway station in Vienna at seven in the evening of May 6, 1942. As the sun set, the passenger train crossed the Danube River with its waters high from the spring run-off. A thousand people were on board — men, women and children. For two days they journeyed through what is now the Czech Republic and Poland. They passed Olmütz, and Neisse, veered east and travelled through Warsaw and Siedlice. And then, late at night on May 8, they reached a town in Byelorussia called Wolkowsk (now known as Volkovysk). There in the darkness, over a period of about three hours, the thousand men, women and children were transferred to freight cars.

The transport started moving again at 2:45 A.M., heading northeast. On the afternoon of the ninth, it arrived at a small place called Koydanov and halted. For forty-two hours the train waited on a siding because of an order given by the security police in Minsk. Eight people died during the layover. Their bodies were taken away and buried nearby.

On May 11, at nine in the morning, the train finally pulled out of Koydanov. It arrived in Minsk an hour and a half later. For my grandparents, Rudolf and Regine, it was the anniversary of a much happier day in May many years before. Twenty-

eight years earlier, their younger son, Günther, had been born on this date.

My children, Rudolf and Regine's great-grandchildren, are yawning now. The fire has begun to die down. Gordon throws on a last log. We are all tired from the drive and the skiing. Though it is still early, we fix hot water bottles and go to bed.

The next day, Saturday, I want to say hello to my mother, so Gordon, Talia and I ski back across the lake to a resort where there is a phone. When my mother doesn't answer, we drive to Lone Butte, a small community nearby. We plan to have something to eat and call again. After lunch we find a phone booth in front of the general store. The Lone Butte Hotel is across the street. Tinsel Christmas garlands still festoon the narrow doorway of the old log structure.

"I had a strange dream," my mother says when we connect. "I was with my daddy, my mommy, your daddy. The children were there. Maybe you and Gordon too. I don't remember what we were doing. But I remember everybody's faces. When I woke up, the phrase 'We are who we are' was in my head."

"I think your daddy was always comfortable with who he was," my mother continues. "It's true he didn't tell you about his background, but I think he was comfortable with not telling you. And when you found out and started to talk to him about it, I think he was comfortable with that too." Talia has something to say, so I pass the phone to her.

Later, as we ski back over the frozen lake, I notice soft spots in the surface. I wonder when break-up will be. And then I hear the geese calling. They are here already, looking for nesting places along the shorelines where the ice has started to melt.

Acknowledgements

This book owes its existence to many people: to my parents, who finally broke their long silence; to my Uncle Günther, who patiently answered so many of my questions; to my husband, Gordon, whose encouragement was unflagging; to my children, Thomas and Talia, whose comments were often very instructive; to my friend Bronia Sonnenschein, who made several valuable suggestions; and to my editor, Barbara Pulling, who had a good way with errant passages.

I am also grateful for the Explorations grant from Canada Council that supported my initial research.

Notes

I have cited most of the written and archival sources of material throughout the text. The following gives some additional sources and more information.

CHAPTER 2
Martin Gilbert's *The Holocaust: A History of the Jews during the Second World War* was published by Holt, Rinehart and Winston, 1985.

CHAPTER 3
George Clare's moving account of the destruction of his family, *Last Waltz in Vienna* (Holt, Rinehart and Winston, 1980) was the source of my information about the violent demonstration in 1927 (pp. 98-99) and the assassination of Dolfuss (pp. 128-34).

The list of countries that were shutting their doors to Jewish refugees came from p. 64 of Martin Gilbert's book *The Holocaust*.

For a description of how the International Settlement was administered, see Marvin Tokayer and Mary Swartz's *The Fugu Plan: The Untold Story of the Japanese and the Jews during World War II* (Paddington Press, 1979), p. 63.

CHAPTER 4

The information that 20,000 Jews were arrested during Kristallnacht comes from a report made by Reinhard Heydrich to Hermann Göring on November 11. It is cited by Raul Hilberg in *The Destruction of the European Jews* (Quadrangle Books, 1961), p. 26. Hilberg points out that the report was incomplete. The final total was undoubtedly higher. I learned that 6500 Jews were taken into custody in Vienna and that 3700 went to Dachau from *Jews, Antisemitism and Culture in Vienna*, edited by I. Oxaal, M. Polak and G. Botz (Routledge & Kegan Paul, 1987), p. 195.

William Shirer describes General Georg von Küchler's arrival in Paris on p. 738 of his book *The Rise and Fall of the Third Reich* (The Reprint Society, 1959).

CHAPTER 6

Karl Frensdorff told me that much of what he knows about the early Frensdorffs came from Dr. S. Gronemann's book *Genealogische Studien über die Alten Jüdische Familien Hannovers* (Louis Lamm, 1913).

William Shirer's remarks about the extent to which Jews were deprived of their livelihood are on p. 233 of his book.

CHAPTER 7

Regina Bruss's comments can be found in *Die Juden unter dem Nationalsozialismus* (Veröffentlichungen aus dem Staatsarchiv der freien Hansestadt Bremen, Bd. 49, 1983), p. 180.

The booklet about Kristallnacht, *Wir Schritten durch eine Schweigende Stadt*, was compiled by Regina Bruss, Ernst Kramer and

Peter Meyer. It is one of a number of booklets published by the Staatsarchiv in Bremen.

Walther Buch's report is mentioned by William Shirer on p. 430.

CHAPTER 8

The source of information about Erwin Schulz's career is Inge Marssolek and Rene Ott's *Bremen im Dritten Reich* (Carl Schünemann Verlag, 1986), pp. 177-78.

For a description of how Jewish immigration to Shanghai was eventually restricted, see David Kranzler's *Japanese, Nazis and Jews: The Jewish Refugee Community of Shanghai 1938-45* (Yeshiva University Press, 1976), pp. 267-76, and Herman Dicker's *Wanderers and Settlers in the Far East* (Twayne Publishers, 1962), pp. 80-97.

To Professor James Ross at Northeastern University in Cambridge, Massachusetts, I am indebted for a list of the ships carrying refugees that arrived in Shanghai between the spring of 1934 and August 1941. It showed that although no German boats landed after August 10, French, Italian, American and Japanese ships did.

CHAPTER 10

From Tess Johnston, who works for the American consulate in Shanghai and has an interest in the history of Europeans in China, I obtained a list of old and new road names in Shanghai. Thus, I know that Bubbling Well Road is now Nanking Road (West), Seymour Road is Shensi Road, the Bund is Chung-Shan Road. I decided, however, to use the street names that were current in the forties since this is how my parents spoke of them.

CHAPTER 11

For an account of the Japanese occupation of the International Settlement in 1941, look at James Vivian Davidson-Houston's *Yellow Creek: The Story of Shanghai* (Putnam, 1962), pp. 171-76.

The method by which Chinese names were transliterated

changed after the Cultural Revolution. But again, I retained the spellings that were current in the forties. Thus, I refer to Soochow Creek, although it is now spelled Suzhou Creek, and to the Whangpoo, which is now written Huangpoo.

A description of how the Japanese closed the *North China Daily News* is contained in Ralph Shaw's *Sin City* (Futura Publications, 1986), pp. 201-4.

CHAPTER 13

Tokayer and Swartz cite the dispatch sent by the Japanese consul on p. 234 of *The Fugu Plan,* and also on that page comment on the first Jewish ghetto in Asia.

Kranzler's remark about the number of Jewish refugees who stayed out of Hongkew is on p. 503 of his book. The proclamation issued by the commanders of the Japanese navy and the army is quoted by Tokayer and Schwartz, Kranzler and Dicker.

CHAPTER 15

My description of August 15, 1945, in Shanghai is based on a March 3, 1993, letter from Roy Essoyan.

CHAPTER 17

I relied on Noel Barber's *The Fall of Shanghai* (MacMillan, 1979) for an account of how the Communists fought their way south from Manchuria.

CHAPTER 18

The term "Shanghailanders" referred to Caucasian residents of Shanghai, "Shanghainese" to the Chinese inhabitants.

The photograph of the nuns is on p. 83 of Sam Tata's *Shanghai – 1949: The End of an Era* (Deneau Publishers, 1990).